Federal Budget

Projections

Studies of Government Finance

TITLES PUBLISHED

Federal Budget

Projections

GERHARD COLM and PETER WAGNER

A Report of the National Planning Association
and the Brookings Institution

Studies of Government Finance

THE BROOKINGS INSTITUTION

WASHINGTON, D.C.

Foreword

THERE IS GENERAL AGREEMENT that the relationship between economic policy planning and budgeting should be improved. Numerous proposals have been made for arrangements that would facilitate the preparation of budgets in the light of economic policy objectives and prospective economic developments. The purpose of this study is to explore the feasibility of interrelating economic and budget estimates by preparing illustrative projections for a ten-year period.

This study has been a joint project of the National Planning Association and the Brookings Institution. It is part of the Brookings series of Studies of Government Finance, a special program of research and education in taxation and government expenditures sponsored by the National Committee on Government Finance. The program is supported with funds provided by the Ford Foundation. A contract with the Department of Labor (in connection with its Study of Economic Growth) also contributed to the resources available for the study.

The authors are members of the staff of the National Planning Association. Gerhard Colm is Chief Economist of the Association and Peter Wagner is a senior staff member.

The authors wish to acknowledge the generous help they received from a considerable number of individuals. For about a year, they had the staff assistance of Eliot Orton and Anthony DeBone. Mrs. Carol Carson read the manuscript and checked it for statistical consistency. In the process of the study individuals at various agencies and particularly the Bureau of the Budget were interviewed. After a first draft was completed it was reviewed by a Reading Committee consisting of Jesse Burkhead of Syracuse University, Samuel

Cohn of the Budget Bureau, and Luther Gulick of the Institute of
Public Administration. Also, Joseph A. Pechman, Brookings' Direc-
tor of Economic Studies, read the manuscript and had comments on
every aspect of the study. Virginia Haaga edited the manuscript and
prepared the index. Each of these reviewers made constructive sug-
gestions on presentation, concepts, and content of the study. The draft
was also reviewed by other members of the Budget Bureau, including
Manuel Helzner, William Ross, and Naomi Sweeney, by Lawrence
Kegan of the Committee for Economic Development, and Jack
Alterman of the Bureau of Labor Statistics. The staff members of
the Budget Bureau commented on conceptual and technical aspects
but refrained from any comments on what programs are included
or excluded in the projections and on any of the estimates. Thus,
the authors take full and exclusive responsibility for the projections.

The views expressed in this volume are those of the authors and
do not purport to represent the views of the Ford Foundation, the
National Committee on Government Finance, or the staff members, officers, or trustees of the Brookings Institution.

Robert D. Calkins
President

December 1965
The Brookings Institution

Preface

THE NATIONAL PLANNING ASSOCIATION issued a Joint Statement on "The Need for Further Budget Reform" in December 1954. This included the following statement:

We propose that, in line with the intent of the Employment Act of 1946, each Economic Report should contain an *economic projection* (including estimates concerning the government sector of the economy) covering a number of years and showing where imbalances might be likely to develop in the national economy. Correspondingly, each Budget Message should contain a *budget outlook* covering the same number of years and demonstrating the changes in expenditures, revenue, and debt policies which would be needed to meet the government's responsibilities under the Employment Act and to promote a better balance in the economy. These estimates would permit deliberation of budget policy for the ensuing year in the longer range perspective of several years, and would help ensure that economic trends were taken into consideration. Experience with informal economic and budget projections made within and without the government justifies the proposal that they be made a regular feature of official documents.

In August 1963 the Joint Economic Committee of Congress made a similar recommendation, and the Budget Bureau has experimented with budget projections under both the Eisenhower and the Kennedy Administrations.

On April 30, 1962, the National Committee on Government Finance of the Brookings Institution asked the National Planning Association to examine the feasibility of making short-term, medium-term, and long-term projections of the federal budget. The study published herewith is a result of this research work. It points out that making such federal budget projections is basically feasible and should be recommended for adoption by the United States government. However, the study also points out that these projections have to be based on specific assumptions with respect to (a) economic developments, and (b) the future development of federal programs and possible changes in tax laws.

With respect to economic development, the government should relate its budget projections primarily to that rate of general economic growth which is held desirable in the national interest. The present study has assumed a rate of growth sufficient to reach reasonably full employment during the fiscal year 1967 and to continue it for the rest of the decade. This would require a rate of growth of about 4 percent, compatible with a rate of unemployment of not more than 4 percent. In order to demonstrate the significance of this assumption the study also presents projections under the assumption of a lesser rate of growth.

Concerning future programs and tax laws the study uses two basic models, namely: (1) continuation of present legislation and policies, including legislation and policies that have been officially recommended by the Administration up to and including those made in the Budget Message of January 1965; and (2) adoption of further changes in programs that have been recommended by responsible and significant groups but not incorporated in official Administration recommendations.

The study involves no procedural difficulty with respect to the first model. The second may raise questions because of possible disagreement about what program changes and changes in tax laws are likely to move into the stage of official consideration over a decade. The authors of the study do not offer this second model as a prediction, nor does it reflect the view of the National Planning Association. However, it would obviously be fallacious to presume that there will be no further additions to or changes in programs and policies over the years. This model remains highly conjectural and "unofficial" but is more likely to be realistic than the model based on a continuation of present policies. In order to allow for the uncertainties with respect to future action, two variations have been computed of this model: one with a larger increase in expenditures and a lesser tax cut, and one with a lesser increase in expenditures and a larger tax cut.

The specific statement of the underlying assumptions and sources of these conjectures will not only forewarn the reader of the projections, but will enable him to modify the model to fit his own conjectures within a balanced framework.

I believe that the study is successful in pointing out both the feasibility and difficulties in making federal budget projections. The authors conclude that projections on both policy assumptions should be made by the Administration as one phase in the process of decision-making. However, they express the view, which I share, that publication of projections which include program and tax changes not yet recommended by the Administration would lead to difficulties and would require a great educational effort before Congress and the public will understand the hypothetical nature of these Model II projections.

In approving this study for publication, the NPA Steering Committee wished me to emphasize in this preface that the authors presented their estimates as illustrations for demonstrating the feasibility and difficulties of such an undertaking. The estimates in no way imply that either the authors or the National Planning Association necessarily recommend the policies incorporated in these projections.

H. Christian Sonne
Chairman, Board of Trustees

December 1965
National Planning Association

Studies of Government Finance

Studies of Government Finance is a special program of research and education in taxation and government expenditures at the federal, state, and local levels. These studies are under the supervision of the National Committee on Government Finance appointed by the trustees of the Brookings Institution, and are supported by a special grant from the Ford Foundation.

MEMBERS OF THE ADVISORY COMMITTEE

Contents

Text Tables

Charts

Appendix Tables

CHAPTER I

Summary and Conclusions

ECONOMIC PROJECTIONS have become one of the major instruments for guidance in public and private decision-making. Business management uses short-term, medium-term, and long-term projections for evaluating future market prospects; it makes projections of the economy as a whole and of its own and its customers' particular branches of business. Labor unions use projections, especially those dealing with the employment outlook and prospective productivity gains, in planning collective bargaining strategy. Government uses economic projections as benchmarks for laying out specific programs (for example, water supply or transportation programs) and for guidance in formulating over-all economic, fiscal, and monetary policy.

The Need for a Study of Budget Projections

Today, government expenditures and revenues are very important factors in all economic projections. Attempts to forecast them involve many difficulties because they are determined not only by long-term economic factors, but also by political factors and economic fluctuations. This is true particularly of the expenditures and receipts of the federal government. Therefore, a detailed exploratory study of projections of the federal budget seems to be useful and timely.

1

Budget projections are desirable for other purposes in addition to their usefulness in making general economic projections. Economists and policy makers have felt for some time that the next year's federal budget could be appraised much more meaningfully if it could be seen in a perspective of several years. This need was emphasized in a statement by the National Planning Association a decade ago[1] and also in a statement of the Committee for Economic Development published in 1962.[2] Recently a subcommittee of the Joint Economic Committee of the United States Congress recommended that the budget for each year should be presented in the context of a broader, longer-run set of budgetary projections, for which a five-year period was thought desirable.[3]

Actually there is no short-term economic forecast that does not incorporate a budget prediction as one of the most important variables. And the intermediate- and long-term economic projections prepared regularly by the National Planning Association[4] and other organizations include projections of expenditures at all levels of government. In 1959 special studies of trends in public expenditures were prepared by Otto Eckstein under the auspices of the CED[5] and by staff members of the NPA.[6] The Budget Bureau itself published five- and ten-year projections in the last days of the Eisenhower Administration.[7] The Budget Bureau regularly puts together five-year budget projections as guides for Executive budget policy, but these projections are for internal use only and are not made public.[8]

[1] *The Need for Further Budget Reform, a Joint NPA Statement* (National Planning Association, 1955).

[2] *Fiscal and Monetary Policy for High Employment* (Committee for Economic Development, 1962).

[3] *The Federal Budget as an Economic Document,* Report of the Subcommittee on Economic Statistics of the Joint Economic Committee, S. Rept. 396, 88 Cong. 1 sess. (1963).

[4] National Planning Association, Center for Economic Projections, *National Economic Projection Series* (issued annually).

[5] Otto Eckstein, *Trends in Public Expenditures in the Next Decade* (Committee for Economic Development, 1959).

[6] Gerhard Colm and Manuel Helzner, "Financial Needs and Resources of the Next Decade: At All Levels of Government," in *Public Finances, Needs, Sources, and Utilization* (Princeton University Press, 1961).

[7] U.S. Bureau of the Budget, *Ten-Year Projections of Federal Budget Expenditures* (Jan. 18, 1961).

[8] Budget Bureau Circular No. A 11 (July 1964) requests from the various agencies program statements and estimates of new obligational authority and of

The present study has a dual purpose. First, it presents a set of up-to-date[9] intermediate- and long-term projections of the federal budget. They were prepared in two steps, presented as Model I and Model II. These estimates were made before defense expenditures were increased for the Viet Nam conflict.

Second, this study attempts to identify the difficulties that are encountered in making such projections and offers recommendations on the feasibility of including medium- and long-term budget projections as a regular feature of the official budget presentation.

Nature of Projections and Assumptions

It should be emphasized that the projections made here are illustrative in character and are in no sense to be regarded as definitive predictions. They indicate the *trend* of expenditures, with the future year indicated (1968 or 1973) serving merely as a benchmark. Fluctuations around the trend line cannot be reflected in the predictions, and periodic revisions are called for to take account of new developments, unforeseen at the time the projections are made.

While projections may be made on either a normative basis—what needs to be done to accomplish certain goals?—or a probability basis—what is most likely to happen?—this study seeks only to estimate *probable* developments, including those resulting from the efforts of government to promote a desirable rate of economic growth.

A difficulty arose in deciding whether to present estimates in constant or in current dollars. Early in the study we came to the conclusion that projections in terms of constant prices were of limited value for medium- and long-term forecasting of budget trends. This is so particularly in the case of revenue projections. While a number of calculations have been made in constant prices for purposes of comparison, most of the detailed figures are shown in current prices, since these give a more realistic picture.

---

expenditures under existing and proposed legislation for three years beyond the next budget year. Thus five years are covered, including the current and the ensuing fiscal years. The five-year projections of the Department of Defense are not comparable with the expenditure estimates for the other agencies.

[9] As of February 1965.

The assumed growth of the American economy, on which our projections are based, is shown in Table 1. (The estimated increase of projected GNP that is believed compatible with the Model I budget projection would fall short of the full employment level of GNP.)

TABLE 1. Models I and II: Gross National Product in Current and Constant Prices, 1963–73

(In billions of current dollars and constant fiscal year 1963 dollars)

Fiscal years	Model I		Model II	
	Current prices	Constant prices	Current prices	Constant prices
Actual				
1963	568.0	568.0	568.0	568.0
1964	604.0	593.9	604.0	593.9
Projected				
1965	640.0	620.8	640.0	620.8
1966	681.5	651.5	681.5	651.5
1967	709.5	669.3	725.3	683.0
1968	739.5	688.5	771.0	715.2
1969	773.0	711.1	813.3	743.4
1970	807.5	733.4	858.0	773.0
1971	844.0	756.3	905.2	803.2
1972	882.0	780.5	955.0	834.8
1973	921.5	804.8	1,007.5	867.8

The estimates in Table 1 are based on the Department of Commerce accounts before the August 1965 revisions of the income and product accounts by economists in the Department. All figures and projections in our study are calculated on the basis of the old estimates. The main conclusions of the study would not be affected by the revisions. If anything, the new figures give further emphasis to our findings. A more detailed explanation of the differences between the two sets of estimates and their implications for the study is given in the introduction to the appendix tables.

Projections are forecasts made under specific, often alternative, assumptions. It is important to state the assumptions explicitly so that a user can modify the projections if he wishes to make different assumptions.

Over-all Assumptions

Certain general assumptions have been made and basic choices taken that are common to all the sets of projections in this study:

1. In the short-term projections (for the fiscal year 1966), the President's proposed budget is used without change.

2. It is assumed that a policy of program expansion will be associated with continuing budget restraint and that, wherever possible, encouragement of private enterprise and support of state-local programs will be preferred to programs operated entirely by the federal government.

3. It is assumed that the Employment Act of 1946 will continue to be a guiding influence for the government and that federal expenditure, tax, credit, and monetary policies will be shaped to support reasonably full employment, adequate economic growth, and reasonable price stability.[10]

4. It is assumed that productivity in government services increases at the same rate as in private activities.

Alternative Models

Presenting very broad ranges of estimates with many alternatives always protects the producer of the estimates but is annoying to the user. Alternatives are often misleading if the reader infers that the most probable value is the mean of the several alternatives, and the projections in this study should not be so interpreted.

MODEL I. The Model I estimates are made under the assumption that no new programs will be adopted, except those already proposed in the 1966 budget,[11] and that there will be no further reductions in tax rates, except for those proposed in the budget for excise taxes. The projections assume that the substantial increase in social security taxes (nearly $5 billion annually) will become effective on January 1, 1966, as proposed.

[10] For exact definitions of these terms, see Model II, below.

[11] Major proposals of the President that are included in the projections but were not yet legislated at the time the manuscript was completed are specified in Chap. VI. The figures include all presidential proposals contained in the fiscal year 1966 budget; later recommendations or congressional amendments could not be taken into account.

Revenues are calculated in Model I on the assumption of a rate of economic growth of 4.4 percent a year, or 3.1 percent in constant dollars. Consistent with this modest rate of growth, a higher and increasing rate of unemployment (5.7 percent for fiscal 1968 and 7 percent for fiscal 1973) has been assumed for this model. Similarly, because of the reduced pressure on resources of all kinds (including labor resources) implied in Model I, we have assumed a price increase of only 1.3 percent annually.

It is also assumed that defense expenditures will remain at a virtually even level, some actual reduction in defense programs being offset by the continuing price rise.

MODEL II. This model includes program changes (additions or cutbacks) and changes in revenue legislation upon which, in the opinion of the authors, decisions are likely to be made during the period under consideration (to 1973). Certainly medium- and long-term projections based only on present legislation and policy proposals would be unrealistic. In the course of the years changes will be proposed and adopted. However, it is unlikely that there will be many changes, at least in the next five years, that are not now being considered informally by the agencies concerned or recommended by various groups. Although predicting *when* these changes are likely to occur is very hazardous, this task has been undertaken in Model II.

The policy changes assumed in Model II should not be understood to be either recommendations or definite forecasts. The estimates have been made to illustrate the problem and to serve as a basis for procedural recommendations. But, tentative as they are, the Model II estimates must be regarded as more realistic than those of Model I, especially for the long-range projections. In a sense, Model I estimates should be regarded as only a phase in the process of making projections rather than as alternative final projections.

Specific assumptions made for Model II are as follows:

1. All Model II estimates assume that the federal government will adopt policies that will reduce unemployment to 4 percent of the civilian labor force during fiscal 1967 and that it will remain at that level for the period covered by the study. It is assumed that

a rate of growth of 4 percent annually in real terms will accomplish this objective once unemployment has been reduced to a 4 percent rate.

2. For the intermediate- and longer-range domestic programs, it is assumed that the war on poverty will be continued and that the federal government will continue to respond to the challenge of great technological possibilities. This implies further emphasis on educational, training, and technological development programs in areas in which private enterprise cannot be expected to perform adequately without government support.

3. All Model II estimates assume that prices will increase at an average annual rate of 1.5 percent and that this will apply to the prices of goods and services bought by the federal government.[12]

Because of the uncertainty about the timing of program expansion, Model II is presented in two variations. Model II-A assumes a smaller increase in expenditures and larger tax cuts; Model II-B assumes a larger increase in expenditures and smaller tax cuts. Model II-A in turn is presented in two combinations, one (II-A1) assuming a virtually constant level of defense expenditures, and the other (II-A2) assuming a substantial reduction in defense expenditures. This introduces a further complication into the projections, as any future reduction in defense programs will probably be associated with a larger increase in nondefense spending, and vice versa.

Summary of Projections

Projections based on President Johnson's proposed budget for 1966 indicate that federal expenditures for nondefense purposes will increase substantially over the level estimated for the fiscal year 1966. Although the President has proposed a number of new programs which would add only relatively small amounts to expenditures in fiscal 1966, they could, if fully implemented, become substantial in later years. Also, the 1966 expenditure estimates were reduced by provision for about $3 billion of receipts from the sale

[12] The increase in prices reflects the average price rise as it is applicable to the GNP as a whole. It is a weighted average of the GNP components. Assuming a continuing increase in the quality of products and services, a 1.5 percent annual price rise may not be inconsistent with the assumption of actual price stability.

of financial assets.[13] Our estimates make only a minor allowance for further liquidation of such assets. This makes the increases in program costs appear somewhat larger than they really are.

This summary will present our projections of total federal receipts and expenditures in terms of the consolidated cash budget. Detailed estimates in terms of the cash budget, as well as of the administrative budget and the federal sector of the national income accounts budget, can be found in Chapter VI and in the appendix tables.

Model I

The assumed rate of growth for Model I (3.1 percent annually) is lower than the 4 percent rate considered to be adequate and assumed for the rest of the models. But even at the 3.1 percent rate, revenues would increase faster than expenditures with some consequent slowdown in the rate of expansion (assuming a relatively restrictive credit policy designed to combat the balance-of-payments deficit). Table 2 shows federal expenditures and receipts under Model I.

The largest expenditure increases under the President's program would occur in social security benefit payments, in education, in health programs, and in the economic opportunity program. In the labor field increased expenditures would be brought about largely by substantially higher unemployment insurance payments under the double impact of improved benefits and a higher unemployment rate due to the slower growth of the economy.

The 1968 budget would still show a small deficit at an unemployment rate of 5.7 percent (as compared with the full employment rate of 4 percent). If this projection were computed under the assumption of full employment (with higher tax yields from full employment income and reduced expenditures because unemployment insurance payments would be lower), it would show some surplus in 1968 and a very large surplus in 1973.

Model I, therefore, is not presented as a real alternative because the very size of the surplus would hinder economic growth, thereby

[13] These include loans held by the Veterans Administration, the Export-Import Bank, the Federal National Mortgage Association, the Small Business Administration, and others.

TABLE 2. Model I: Cash Budget, 1963, 1966, 1968, and 1973[a]

(In billions of current dollars for fiscal years)

Item	Actual 1963	Proposed 1966	Projected	
			1968	1973
Gross national product	568.0	681.5	739.5	921.5
Expenditures				
Defense	53.4	52.5	52.8	53.3
Other	60.4	74.9	89.0	114.4
Total	113.8	127.4	141.8	167.7
Receipts	109.7	123.5	(137.9)[b]	(175.2)[b]
Excess of receipts (+)	−4.0	−3.9	(−3.9)	(+7.5)[c]

Note: Details may not add to totals due to rounding.

[a] In this and the following tables, all figures for fiscal year 1963 are actual; those listed as "proposed 1966" are the officia lestimates of the 1966 budget; and those listed as "projections" for 1968 and 1973 are based on our own assumptions for the particular model as given in the text and in Table 1.

[b] The revenue estimates do not take account of possible further tax reductions. Figures in parentheses are estimates that appear unrealistic without assuming tax reductions beyond those proposed in the 1966 budget. See text for a discussion of assumptions on which the various models are based.

[c] See the text for comments about the effects of this surplus on the rate of growth

leading to rising unemployment and forcing the government to adopt either an increase in programs or a reduction in tax rates or a combination of both in order to achieve a higher rate of economic growth and to reduce unemployment. The existence of this surplus (combined with a fairly restrictive monetary policy) would probably be incompatible with sustaining even the inadequate rate of growth assumed for this model.

Model II

The new and expanded nondefense programs assumed in Model II are specified in Part II. The principal new programs assumed to come up for debate and adoption during the coming decade are in the domestic field and concern housing, health, research, education and training, and the economic opportunity programs, as well as improvements in the social insurance programs. All of them are programs that have been recommended by some groups but are not included in present official proposals. Model II-A makes relatively small allowances for these new and expanded programs, and Model

TABLE 3. Model II Under Various Assumptions—II-A1, II-A2, and II-B—Cash Budget, 1963, 1966, 1968, and 1973[a]

(In billions of current dollars for fiscal years)

Item	Actual 1963	Proposed 1966	Model II-A1 Projections		Model II-A2 Projections		Model II-B Projections	
			1968	1973	1968	1973	1968	1973
Gross national product	568.0	681.5	771.0	1,007.5	771.0	1,007.5	771.0	1,007.5
Expenditures								
Defense	53.4	52.5	52.8	53.3	49.7	43.5	49.7	43.5
Other	60.4	74.9	93.7	129.0[b]	93.6	129.0[b]	103.3	155.0
Total	113.8	127.4	146.5	182.3	143.3	172.5	153.0	198.5
Receipts	109.7	123.5	(146.4)[c]	(198.4)[c]	(146.4)[c]	(198.4)[c]	146.4	199.7
Excess of receipts (+)	−4.0	−3.9	(−0.1)	(+16.1)[d]	(+3.1)	(+25.9)[d]	(−6.6)	+1.2

Note: Details may not add to totals due to rounding.
[a] Model II-A1 assumes present defense programs; II-A2 and II-B, substantially reduced defense programs.
[b] For an explanation of interest calculations on the federal debt, see Chap. X.
[c] The revenue estimates do not take account of possible further tax reductions. Figures in parentheses are estimates that appear unrealistic without assuming tax reductions beyond those proposed in the 1966 budget. See text for a discussion of assumptions on which the various models are based.
[d] See the text for comments about the effects of this surplus on the rate of growth.

10

II-B allows for increases of considerable size. Projected expenditures and receipts under the two versions of Model II-A and under Model II-B are shown in Table 3.

In both Models II-A and II-B the adoption of new programs and some expansion of most existing programs beyond present or proposed legislation have been assumed; expenditures for space and agriculture, however, would be reduced. Under the stimulus of additional programs the economy would grow at a higher rate, and revenues would increase correspondingly faster. Some further cut in taxes by 1968 and a substantial reduction by 1973 would be feasible and necessary to support the rate of growth posited for Model II-A1. In the case of Model II-A2 (the arms-reduction model) an earlier and more substantial tax cut would be necessary. By 1973 a modest tax cut might be advisable for Model II-B as well. These reductions could take the form either of a lowering of federal tax rates or of a sharing of federal revenues with state and local governments so that they could reduce their taxes or increase their expenditures without state and local tax increases.

Model II-B assumes adoption of the same new or expanded nondefense programs as in Model II-A but with considerably larger amounts. However, this model seems realistic only if a substantial reduction in defense expenditures is assumed. Therefore, this substantial increase in nondefense expenditures is not combined (as it is in Model II-A) with another variation showing a continued high level of defense expenditures. Whether in this case, in addition to the large increase in nondefense expenditures, a relatively small cut in taxes or transfer to state-local governments would also be possible depends on the development of the other sectors in the economy. However, such transfers would be less urgent, as this model assumes very substantial increases in federal grants-in-aid to state and local governments.

Conclusions

From a comparison of these various models some obvious conclusions can be drawn:

1. If the programs initiated or proposed in recent years are implemented by adequate appropriations and administrative policies, federal expenditures are likely to increase year by year by consider-

able amounts. This will be true even if some programs are implemented only slowly.

2. The increase in economic activities (combined with a very small increase in prices) will result in an increase in revenues in excess of that projected in expenditures. The automatic increase in receipts (including social security taxes) resulting from a 5.5 percent economic growth (in current dollars), under present tax legislation, will amount to somewhat more than $7 billion a year. For the period 1968-73 it is estimated at about $10 billion. There will also be a "built-in" increase in expenditures resulting from the development in existing programs, the price rise, service of the national debt, and other factors. Under present legislation this automatic increase might be estimated at over $3 billion a year. If adoption and implementation of the Great Society program in full is assumed, the built-in increase may amount to over $6 billion a year. This means that under existing and proposed legislation the automatic increase in revenue would exceed the built-in increase in expenditures by an average of $3 to $4 billion each year for the period 1968-73. If it is assumed that in a base period the full employment budget is in balance with other economic factors, this would mean that each year there would be room for some increase in programs or initiation of new programs, some reduction in tax rates, some possible sharing of funds with state and local governments, or some combination of these. In fact, it would be necessary to give effect to some or all of these measures in order to achieve and maintain full employment in future years.

3. The size of the tax reduction that will be possible (and needed if a depressing effect on the economy is to be avoided) will depend on the size and pace of the expansion of federal expenditure programs.

4. None of our models shows a ratio of federal expenditures to the gross national product (GNP) assumed for the same period that is higher than that of fiscal year 1963, and most alternatives remain substantially below that level. (See Table 4.)

Chart 1 shows the projected rate of growth of federal cash expenditures (in constant dollars) in the perspective of the past 35 years and also in relation to the actual and projected GNP. It shows that the estimates made here, even though they were not obtained by extrapolation, are in line with the historical experience of periods in which no major emergency occurred.

For an economic evaluation of present and proposed programs, and those under consideration, it should be remembered that some grants, particularly those concerned with transportation, housing, health, welfare, economic opportunity, and education call for matching by the states so that in many cases they would involve additional state or local, as well as federal, expenditures. Also some of the programs, particularly the various housing loan programs, Export-Import Bank, and Commodity Credit Corporation loans, as well as many others, provide for federal guarantee or in-

TABLE 4. Model I and Model II: Federal Expenditures as a Percentage of Gross National Product, Cash Budget, Fiscal Years 1963, 1966, 1968, and 1973

Item	1963	1966	1968	1973
Actual expenditures	20.0			
Proposed expenditures		18.7		
Projected expenditures in:				
Model I			19.2	18.2
Model II-A1			19.0	18.1
Model II-A2			18.6	17.1
Model II-B			19.8	19.7

surance of loans issued by private enterprise or state and local governments. These would add only very small amounts to federal budgetary expenditures. In addition many agencies use their receipts from the public as revolving funds, and only their net expenditures are reflected in the budget. These examples are given to show that the operations of the federal government have a considerably greater impact on the nation's economy than a brief glance at the budget figures alone would suggest.

Procedural Recommendations

This study was undertaken because of the conviction that intermediate- and long-term budget projections are needed as elements in intermediate- and long-term economic projections and to provide perspective for evaluating the budget for the ensuing year. Given

CHART 1. Federal Cash Payments to the Public, Fiscal Years 1929–66, and Projected 1968 and 1973, in Dollars and as a Percentage of GNP[a]

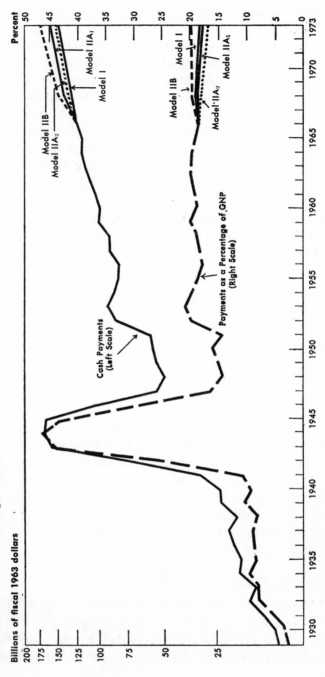

[a] As a percentage of calendar year GNP, 1929–41; as a percentage of fiscal year GNP, 1942–73.

14

the present character of government programs, it is nonsensical to think in terms of a 365-day budget. The problem posed for the present study was not whether or not intermediate- and long-term budget projections are desirable; nor did we need a study to prove that making longer-term budget projections is a hazardous undertaking. By preparing projections we hoped to gain insight into the specific difficulties one encounters and to explore ways to overcome or reduce the difficulties and hazards. Although the validity of our projections can be tested only by comparison with actuals at a future time, we submit the following tentative conclusions from our experience:

1. From this effort to project budget expenditures and revenues for intermediate- and long-term periods (five and ten years) ahead it appears that it is feasible to make meaningful projections.

2. The Budget Bureau could probably make more reliable estimates if other government agencies were given more specific guidelines and would devote a greater effort to the preparation of their own budget projections. They also should submit a list of program proposals that are under serious discussion in their areas of responsibility even though these are not yet officially recommended by the President. The Budget Bureau should not, however, merely collect and compile the agency estimates but should evaluate them and especially should appraise new program proposals for which no specific agency is currently responsible. The Budget Bureau should also identify programs that may be terminated or curtailed.

3. Giving the various agencies and their subdivisions responsibility for medium- and long-term budget projections is important because thinking in these longer-run terms will have a desirable effect on the attitude of the officials concerned.

4. It is important to formulate broad assumptions with respect to the political and economic situations, both international and domestic. Projections will always remain hypothetical in character. The assumptions should be formulated in interagency consultations and communicated to all officials concerned with the preparation of projections.

5. It is assumed that federal budget policy will be used as one of the tools for attaining the general economic objectives of developing the nation's potential resources, approximating full em-

ployment, and maintaining reasonable price stability. Therefore, budget projections should be related to, and integrated with, general economic projections. This will require cooperation between the Budget Bureau and the Council of Economic Advisers.

6. Budget projections should first be prepared on the basis of existing policies and official policy proposals for a five-year period. In addition, it would be desirable to prepare another set of estimates to include those changes in expenditure programs and tax legislation which are only under consideration but which are likely to be adopted within the projection period. It becomes increasingly important to include program and tax changes beyond those officially proposed when longer time periods are covered by the projections. For estimates going beyond the five-year period, this procedure becomes absolutely necessary. Alternative projections may be useful in this situation. Projections that allow for program and tax changes that are not yet officially proposed should be clearly identified in order to avoid any confusion between officially proposed program and tax changes and those that have merely received unofficial consideration.

7. It is useful to build up the projections from considerable agency detail. However, details should be presented only by broad functional classifications. The longer the period for which projections are made, the fewer details should be given.

8. It is recognized that any projections released by the federal government will arouse controversy. This is so especially in the case of projections similar to our Model II, which envisage the possibility of new legislation initiating some expenditure programs or terminating others, or imply that changes in tax legislation might be adopted in the future. Publication of such hypothetical projections might present difficulties for federal agencies, because including these changes might make it appear that the administration was proposing that they be made. Before a projection of this kind is included in official documents, Congress and the public should become more familiar with such projections. The inclusion of program changes that are not yet approved has the advantage that it may stimulate a public debate before an official recommendation is made. For a strictly transitional period it might be advisable to limit the publication of projections by the Bureau of the Budget to

five-year projections based on existing and officially proposed legislation only.

9. For these reasons, a research organization not connected with the federal government might fulfill a very real and necessary educational function in preparing and publishing independent projections of federal revenues and expenditures, particularly longer-term ones. Because of the controversial nature of these projections, and in order to facilitate intelligent discussion, it might be desirable to continue the preparation and publication of such private estimates even after the federal government has begun to publish projections on a regular basis.

10. Any such projections, whether originating within or outside the federal government, would have to be revised and updated on a continuing basis in the light of changing circumstances if they are to furnish reliable guidance to economic policy-makers in business and government.

11. Projections have to be worked out on a year-by-year basis. Publication of intermediate- and longer-term estimates may be confined to a smaller number of benchmark years. It is recognized that individual years would deviate from such a trend line.

12. For the purpose of integrating budget projections with general economic projections, and to facilitate a comparison with the national income accounts, the definition and terminology of the object classification contained in the budget document and the national income usages of these terms must be more closely aligned. At present the definitions are not closely related. In addition, it would help if the object classification in the budget document were computed and published on an expenditure basis, and not only on an anticipated new obligational authority basis, which is the practice at present. A classification of government functions that distinguishes current operations from programs designed to support the future productivity and growth of the economy would be desirable.

13. We feel that at the agency level it is generally not desirable for the same persons to be engaged both on current work and on budget projections covering future years. When one is immersed in budget detail, it is exceedingly hard to divorce oneself sufficiently from current pressures to retain an imaginative outlook regarding future needs and possible developments.

For these reasons, it is suggested that the task of making such projections might be assigned to special program officers at the agency level, and to an expanded section of the Bureau of the Budget which would be concerned with broad government programs. Of course, in all cases, close cooperation with the budget officers in each agency and with the Budget Bureau examiners would have to be established.

14. These recommendations would mean a heavier workload for the Bureau of the Budget, and its staff would have to be increased somewhat. Similarly, a limited number of additional persons would be necessary in other agencies.

All projections of budget receipts and expenditures must allow for a great number of variables, the effects of which can only be estimated. Ultimately, new computer techniques would be of considerable help in this. For example, it may not be too fanciful to hope that eventually a computer bank could be established capable of storing and processing budget and economic data to indicate broadly what effects any given combination of expenditure and tax policies might have on any major sector of the American economy. Federal budget projections would be indispensable in this case, and a considerable number of policy alternatives could be explored in this fashion.

PART ONE

Problems in Budget Projections

CHAPTER II

The Feasibility of
Budget Projections

STATEMENTS ABOUT THE future are more than "hunches" only if they are based on observations of the past and the present. A budget proposal reflects the political program of an administration; the budget actually adopted reflects, in addition, the political situation in Congress. Thus it might appear that a projection of the budget for 1968 or 1973 would depend entirely on a forecast of the political climate in 1968 and 1973. If this were the case, budget projections for future years would be a task for political soothsayers. Some skeptics deny the feasibility of longer-term budget projections on these grounds.

Determinants of Future Budgets

Actually there is a more solid basis for budget projections as long as it is assumed that no drastic changes will take place in either the international or the domestic political situation. For one thing, many decisions determining the 1973 budget are made in prior years. Earlier legislation and contractual obligations determine a large portion of expenditures. In other cases expenditures are continued because they can be reduced only by wasteful termination of going programs. Sometimes changes that are made in expenditures are more apparent than real as, for example, when a reduction is achieved by shifting from direct government loans to a federal guarantee of private or local government loans or by selling financial assets.[1]

The *pace* of program expansion is more subject to political control. Nevertheless, the *probability* of future program expansion can, to some extent, be discovered in advance. Except in emergency situations, the adoption of new programs, the expansion or contraction of old ones, or changes in tax legislation are usually preceded by several years of debate. In the Model II estimates no new or expanded programs are included that have not been debated and recommended by responsible groups of experts.

Finally, and most important, whether or not the government undertakes particular programs is not decided arbitrarily. The underlying forces are determined by economic, social, and technological developments. For example:

• When some population groups or regions do not participate in a rapid rise of general well-being, it is only a matter of time until the government is concerned with the problem. It is also recognized as the government's responsibility to promote economic growth and the creation of job opportunities, which are probably the most effective means of combating poverty in general.

• When revolutionary technological developments make old skills obsolescent and require new skills, the government responds with enlarged training programs. Previously, efforts were made through relief and assistance programs to mitigate the distress of families which, for reasons beyond their own control, could not make ends meet. To these are being added education and training programs designed to increase the employment potential and earning power of people who are able to work.

• When greater affluence and increased bargaining power of labor is achieved, the need for government assistance in some instances may be reduced. For instance, the spectacular spread of private group health insurance for employees has developed into a partial alternative to a general social health insurance system.

• When metropolitan or megalopolitan transportation needs ex-

[1] For an explanation of the latter, see pages 7-8.

ceed what private enterprise or local government can meet, sooner or later the federal government will embark on a program to support rapid mass transportation.

• When science opens new frontiers in space, or in oceans, or in energy resources which cannot be developed by private business alone, it is a safe guess that the government will not permit these possibilities to remain unexploited.

• When nonfarm employment opportunities for marginal farmers expand, it may be possible to reduce the large farm subsidy programs. A declining political influence of farm interests (for example, by reapportionment) would reduce possible obstacles to a more efficient organization of farm programs.

• When rising income and profits result in a faster increase in tax revenues than in expenditures, thus exerting a "fiscal drag" on economic growth and rising employment opportunities, sooner or later tax rates will be reduced.

We do not suggest that political decisions of the future can be rigidly determined in the light of current technological, economic, and social developments. Political leadership certainly can and does influence the pace and character of the government response to these developments. Therefore, the projection of a trend, in which a future year merely serves as a benchmark, is more meaningful than a prediction for any specific year. Also it is less risky to state that the government is likely to support a certain development than to predict the exact institutional form such support is likely to take. Projections on specific policies can be based only on debates that have already taken place. However, the time lag between a challenge by social, economic, and technological factors on the one hand, and the response by debate, formulation, proposal, adoption, and implementation of government programs on the other, creates the basis for budget projections that are not merely political speculations.

The Historical Trend

The simplest method of projection is to extrapolate past trends. If there were a long period of "normal" development in the past and a foreseeable period of "normal" development ahead, this might be a good method. The past fifty years have been anything but normal, however. They included two world wars, several localized conflicts, a great depression, a dissolution of a world order, the emergence of many new sovereign states, and profound changes in the domestic political, social, economic, and technological environment of government operation.

At the beginning of the twentieth century, federal government expenditures amounted to $500 million or, expressed in present dollar values, to about $2.25 billion, and increased to $120 billion (consolidated cash account) in 1964—or almost sixty times. As a percentage of GNP they grew from around 3 percent to nearly 20 percent during the same period. Federal revenues showed a similar rise.[2]

The trend of federal expenditures and revenues shows a clear pattern. In the period from 1900 until the United States entered World War I in 1917, federal expenditures and revenues grew, but expanded less rapidly than did the economy as a whole. The war and immediate postwar period saw a radical transformation, with expenditures rising to 20 percent of GNP and taxes increasing substantially. During the twenties, federal expenditures and revenues declined from the war and immediate postwar level but remained far above the prewar level, both in dollars and in their relation to GNP.

Again expenditures rose rapidly during the depression of the thirties—mostly as a result of programs designed to combat mass unemployment. Revenues declined during this period. In 1940 federal expenditures amounted to 9 percent of GNP. During World War II they approximated $100 billion, or 46 percent of GNP. High wartime tax rates and economic expansion resulted in large increases in revenues. After 1945, federal expenditures and revenues were drastically reduced but again remained at more than double the prewar level (in constant prices).

This pattern was repeated on a smaller scale during and after the Korean War. Expenditures rose slowly but consistently from 1955 to 1960, and at an accelerated rate from 1961 to 1964. However, the rate of increase was less during 1964. They remained at a relatively constant percentage (below 20 percent) of the growing GNP.

[2] See Chart 1 and Table 4 in Chap. I.

The pattern of federal expenditure development is less erratic if programs for defense and war liquidation are excluded. Chart 2 shows the development of the administrative budget during the years 1900-64. Chart 3 shows the development for major nonwar-related expenditures and governmental functions of the administrative budget during the period 1913-64.

Nondefense domestic expenditures of the federal government were below 1 percent of GNP in the period before the great depression. During that emergency period they were raised temporarily to 7 percent of GNP. The drastic cutback during World War II is not shown in the chart because civilian agencies (such as the Maritime Commission) had large war-related expenditures that appear in the nondefense category. After the war, these expenditures moved gradually from 2 percent of GNP in the fiscal year 1948 to almost 4 percent in fiscal 1964. On a per capita basis, these expenditures, again in constant dollars, did not reach the level of the emergency year 1939 until fiscal 1964, as shown in Chart 3.

This brief review of past trends in federal revenues and expenditures suggests that during periods of peacetime development the nation's ideas concerning the appropriate levels of expenditures and taxation and the share of total GNP going to the federal government through taxes tend to change only slowly. Only clearly recognizable "emergency" situations have made substantial deviations from the previous norm acceptable.

During this century such emergencies have arisen during the two World Wars, the Korean War, and the great depression of the thirties, the latter having been important mainly for expenditures. During the war periods the American public accepted increased levels of taxation as a national necessity, and, although in each instance there was some lowering of tax levels after the emergency had passed, they remained considerably higher than those prevailing before the upheaval. The public had become reconciled to permanently higher levels of taxation, not indeed because of any great love of taxes, but rather because during the emergency periods political and psychological obstacles to increased government responsibilities and increased taxes were overcome.

This experience holds important lessons for the projections here because it is assumed that no "emergency" will occur during the

CHART 2. Federal Expenditures and Receipts, Administrative Budget, 1900–64, in Dollars and as a Percentage of GNP

Billions of fiscal 1963 dollars

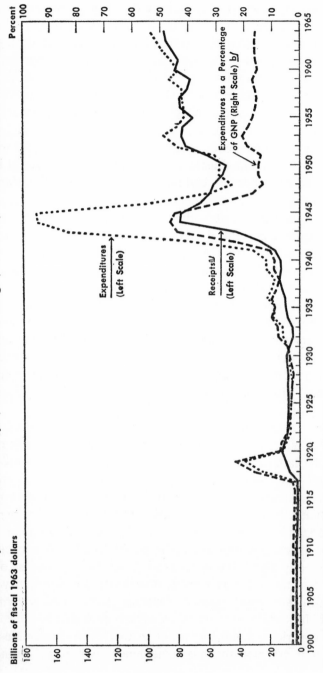

Expenditures
(Left Scale)

Receipts a/
(Left Scale)

Expenditures as a Percentage
of GNP (Right Scale) b/

Percent

Source: Current dollar data, *The Budget in Brief, Fiscal Year 1966* (1965).
a Prior to 1931, total receipts, thereafter net receipts.
b As a percentage of GNP average for two- and four-year periods, 1900–18; as a percentage of calendar year GNP, 1919–41; as a percentage of fiscal year GNP thereafter.

26

period covered by the study. This applies both to the international situation, where the alternatives assume a continuation of the present situation or a slight further easing of tensions, and certainly to the domestic scene, where fairly prosperous conditions are assumed. Our projections assume that programs expand in line with population growth and in response to the social challenges of growing economic capacity and technological possibilities.

The peculiar history of the past fifty years excludes extrapolation as a method of projecting federal expenditures into the future. However, the plausibility of the projections made here can be tested in the light of historical experience. Searching questions must be asked and answered if a projection made under the assumption of "normal" conditions shows an increase in federal expenditures and taxes larger than the rate of general economic expansion. Certainly there is no absolute ceiling that can be pierced only under emergency conditions, but in the absence of an emergency, the urgency of additions to federal programs must be very clear to the political leadership and the citizenry.

Actually the projections in this study do not imply an increase in the proportion of GNP absorbed by federal expenditures. If some reduction in defense expenditures proves possible, the proportion of GNP absorbed will decline, and a substantial tax reduction should be possible. Thus, while the projections are not obtained by extrapolation of historical trends, they do not appear unrealistic in the light of historical experience.[3]

U.S. Experience with Budget Projections

Probably the first official long-term projection of federal expenditures was prepared in 1944 for the postwar period. At that time various private proposals for postwar tax reform were being discussed which assumed postwar expenditures of $16-$18 billion (compared with less than $9 billion before World War II and $100 billion in fiscal 1945). Sometime in 1944 President Roosevelt asked the Budget Bureau to prepare an estimate of the likely level of federal expenditures in the postwar period.[4] In a discussion of "The

[3] See Chart 1.
[4] Reported from memory by the senior author.

CHART 3. Federal Domestic Nondefense Expenditures,[a] Administrative Budget, Fiscal Years, 1913–64: Total Expenditures, Per Capita Expenditures, and Expenditures as a Percentage of GNP

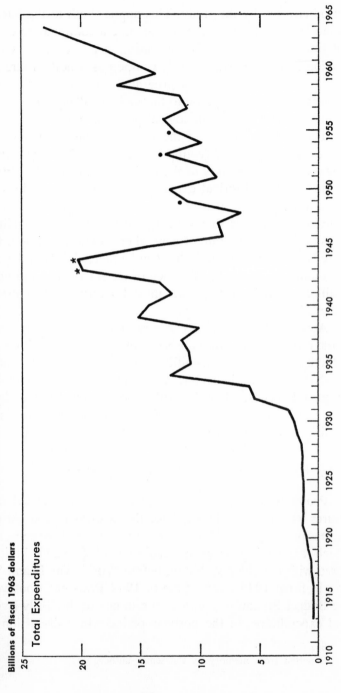

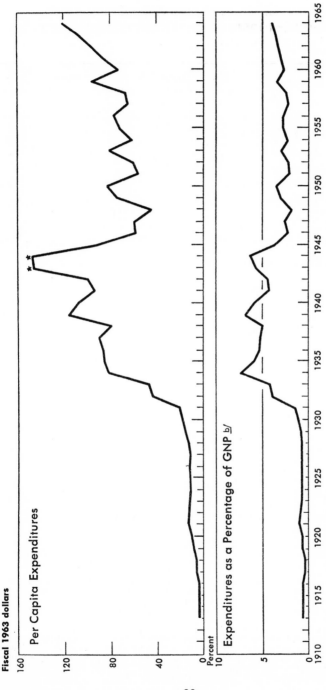

Fiscal 1963 dollars

160

Per Capita Expenditures

120

80

40

0

Percent

10

Expenditures as a Percentage of GNP b/

5

1910   1915   1920   1925   1930   1935   1940   1945   1950   1955   1960   1965

* Includes war activities of nondefense agencies.
● Includes especially large increases in agriculture and agricultural resources, combined with increases of a smaller magnitude in other functions.

Sources: Bureau of the Census, *Historical Statistics of the United States* (1960); *Economic Report of the President, 1965; The Budget in Brief, Fiscal Year 1966* (1965).
a Defined as total administrative budget expenditures less the functional categories of national defense, international affairs, veterans' benefits, and services, and interest.
b As a percentage of average GNP for two- and four-year periods, 1913–18; as a percentage of calendar year GNP, 1919–41; as a percentage of fiscal year GNP thereafter.

29

TABLE 5. Summary of Selected Budget Projections Prepared in 1959 and 1961

(In billions of dollars)

Date prepared, source, and form of projection	Year projected for	Original projection	Inflator[a]	Inflated projection	Actual
Prepared April 1959 in 1958 prices:					
Colm-Helzner[b]	Calendar 1964				
Federal expenditures, national income		101.9	115.0	117.2	119.2
State-local expenditures, national income		64.6	120.5	77.8	67.3
Eckstein[c]	Fiscal 1964				
Federal cash budget expenditures		106.2	112.3	119.3	120.3
Federal administrative budget expenditures		88.0	112.3	98.8	97.7
State-local expenditures, national income (excluding grants-in-aid)		47.4	118.2	56.0	54.8
Prepared October 1959 in 1958 prices:					
National Planning Association[d]	Calendar 1965				
Total government purchases of goods and services		125.0	121.7	152.1	135.6
Prepared January 1961 in fiscal 1960 prices:					
Bureau of the Budget[e]	Fiscal 1965				
Federal administrative budget expenditures		88.8	111.8	99.3	96.5

[a] The original projections were made in prices of a base period. The inflator is used to adjust the original projections to the price level of the actuals, so that the inflated projections and the actuals are comparable. (See also footnote e.)

[b] Gerhard Colm and Manuel Helzner, "Financial Needs and Resources Over the Next Decade: at All Levels of Government," in Universities-National Bureau of Economic Research, *Public Finances: Needs, Sources, and Utilization* (Princeton University Press, 1961), p. 8. Judgment projection.

[c] Otto Eckstein, *Trends in Public Expenditures in the Next Decade* (Committee for Economic Development, April 1959), pp. 6 and 9. Medium projection.

[d] National Planning Association, *Long-Range Projections for Economic Growth* (1959), p. 6. Judgment projection.

[e] U. S. Bureau of the Budget, *Ten-Year Projections of Federal Budget Expenditures* (1961), p. 3. Medium projection. This projection includes $3 billion for pay raises for civilian, military, and postal employees. Since the inflator for government expenditures makes no provision for productivity increases so that the total pay increase is reflected as a price rise, there is some double counting. Were adjustments made, the inflated projection would be several billion dollars lower. The same qualification applies to the other projections.

Government's Budget and the Nation's Budget," in the budget message for fiscal 1946 (issued in January 1945), the President asked, "What will be the outlook when Federal expenditures are 50 and 25 billion dollars in the period of demobilization and thereafter?"[5] This implies a projection of a $25 billion federal budget after the demobilization period. Perhaps the $25 billion should be compared with the actual for the fiscal year 1950, which was after demobilization and before the Korean War rearmament. The $25 billion, expressed in 1944 prices, corresponds to about $35 billion in fiscal 1950 prices and compares with the actual of $39.5 billion for that year.

The National Planning Association's *National Budgets for Full Employment* (prepared in 1944 and published in 1945) also made a projection for 1950.[6] Federal expenditures for goods and services (at that time conceptually including debt service) were projected in the models to lie between $18 billion and $25 billion in 1941 prices. Adjusted for price changes and to exclude interest, the range would be $20-$30 billion, compared to the actual expenditure of $19.3 billion. State-local expenditures were estimated at $9.6 billion, corresponding to $17.4 billion in 1950 prices; this compares with an actual figure of $19.7 billion.

Several projections of government expenditures were prepared by private organizations (in 1959) and the Bureau of the Budget (published in 1961) for the years 1964 and 1965, as mid-points in ten-year projections. Table 5 compares the projections with actuals (or estimated actuals). While none of the projections was precisely accurate, they are not useless as a general guide. However, periodic revisions are needed to achieve greater accuracy.

Foreign Experience with Budget Projections

Other countries of the Western world have also found it useful to prepare intermediate- and longer-term budget projections. In a number of countries the government presents economic plans or national budgets necessitating official budget projections.

[5] U.S. Bureau of the Budget, *The Budget of the United States Government* (1945), p. xxiv.

[6] The pamphlet notes the year as 195X, but the demographic figures cited make it clear that the authors had the year 1950 in mind.

In Great Britain the government presented to Parliament in December 1963, a paper entitled "Public Expenditure in 1963/64 and 1967/68." The paper gave an estimate of the major categories of expenditures "at 1963 prices on the basis of the Government's present policies and programmes"[7] and envisaged a rise of 17.5 percent for such expenditures over the four-year period. It also contained a comparison with prospective resources based on an assumed 4 percent annual increase in GNP.

In France the five-year plan also includes official estimates of government outlays on current and capital account, the most recent ones covering the years 1966-70. The tentative estimates of the plan are discussed in the legislature before they are made final. A "perspective" for 1985 has been prepared by a working group set up by the government at the end of 1962 to provide a general background for the Fifth Plan. This perspective suggests that, assuming an average rate of growth of 4.7 percent for the economy as a whole from 1960 to 1985, the government capital account expenditures—including agricultural, urban, school, cultural, health, highway, telephone, research, and other investments—will rise from 8 billion francs in 1960 and 14 billion francs in 1965 to between 40 and 60 billion francs in today's prices in 1985, or 6.6 to 8.4 percent a year.[8]

For the Netherlands a special Commission for a Revision of the Budget Law recommended in September 1960 that a general budgetary plan for several years ahead should be published regularly in the "Budget Memorandum," which is the introduction to the Annual Budget.

In Canada the Royal Commission on Government Organization recommended in 1962:

> . . . that all departments and agencies be required to prepare and submit to the Executive long-term plans of expenditure requirements by programmes. Based thereon, an over-all forecast of government expenditures and prospective resources for a period of five years ahead [should] be prepared annually.[9]

[7] Cmnd. 2235 (London: Her Majesty's Stationery Office, December 1963), p. 5.

[8] *Reflexions Pour 1985 (La Documentation Française,* Paris, 1964), p. 66.

[9] Quoted in Economic Council of Canada, *First Annual Review: Economic Goals for Canada to 1970* (Ottawa: Queen's Printer, December 1964), p. 194.

The Economic Council of Canada repeated this recommendation in its report of December 1964 and included a projection of total expenditures of all levels of government by function for 1970. In explaining the projections the Council said:

These estimates are based primarily upon the existing complex of policies, the probable increases associated with population change, and upon continuing trends towards improved standards. No account is taken, however, of any major new policy developments except where these have been generally or explicitly indicated by governments, or where significantly increased levels of expenditure appear appropriate either to the requirements for, or as a consequence of, expansion of the economy to potential output.

... the projections ... are not in any way intended to represent either a forecast of probable government expenditures by 1970, or a portrayal of an optimum pattern from any particular point of view. They indicate rather the general order of magnitude of expenditure programmes by function which might be expected to emerge under conditions of rapid economic growth.[10]

This description characterizes well the kind of projections the present study tries to illustrate. There is, of course, no intention of suggesting that what is desirable and feasible in another country must also be desirable and feasible in the United States. Political conditions are very different under a parliamentary system than under one in which the legislative power is divided between the President and the Congress.

In spite of existing political difficulties in the public use of official budget projections, judging by the experience with the projections made here and with previous less detailed projections and by the practice in other countries, it is feasible to prepare medium- and long-term budget projections and to present them for public debate. They are, of course, subject to error and should be revised periodically in the light of political, economic, and technological developments. To quote the Canadian Royal Commission again: "A five-year projection, amended and updated each year, should be an indispensable tool for policy-making. . . ."[11]

[10] *Ibid.*, p. 115.
[11] *Ibid.*, p. 194.

CHAPTER III

Method of Budget Projections

WITH THE GROWING importance of the federal budget for the development of the economy an old dilemma becomes of increasing importance. The larger the public interest in budgets the greater becomes the need to adopt simple, generally understandable concepts and methods of calculation. At the same time, however, the growing complexity of the relationship between the public and private sectors of the economy makes it necessary to use various methods of budget projections and various concepts. While we have made an effort at simplification, there is still the problem that budget projections can serve different purposes and that different purposes require different concepts and methods of computation.

Character of the Projections: Normative and Probability Elements

Projections can have either a normative or a probability character.[1] In the first case they establish a target that needs to be

[1] The dichotomy between normative and probability projections is an oversimplification. Most important for planning purposes are what may be called

hit if certain desirable objectives are to be attained. For example, the question could be asked: assuming that an average annual long-term rate of growth of about 4 percent is desirable for the American economy, what federal budget policy would be needed to support this objective?

In the case of a probability projection the question asked is not what budget policy is needed in support of an objective, but what is the likely future development of budget expenditures and revenues in the light of probable economic, social, and political influences.

Actually the two approaches are not entirely independent of each other. The federal government is committed by the Employment Act—and by sheer political necessity—to a policy that will promote conditions favorable to high employment, economic growth, price stability, and international competitiveness. Therefore, it is *probable* that it will pursue a budget policy aimed at promoting these objectives. Thus, a normative factor enters into the probability projection of budgets.

There is also the other relationship. In setting goals, for instance, for a desirable rate of growth, consideration is given to the benefits derived from a high rate of growth and obstacles to policies needed to achieve a high rate of growth. Why then has discussion in recent years about a desirable annual rate of growth in the United States centered on a range of 3.5 to 5.0 percent, instead of the higher rates debated in other countries? The reason is that higher rates of growth would probably require the adoption of policies that the American public would consider unacceptable in peacetime. Thus a probability also enters into the establishment of a target.

There still remains a difference between a normative and a probability projection, however. It is assumed in the latter that objectives will be pursued, but it is considered probable that the objective (for instance, a very low rate of unemployment) will not quite be accomplished. Thus, the probability projection allows for some "slippage," which is not allowed for in the target or normative pro-

---

operational projections. They incorporate estimates which in case of error minimize the harm when used for operational purposes. Assume, for example, that at the beginning of a war, a short war is believed most probable. Nevertheless, it may be safer to estimate requirements for a longer war. This criterion may lead to a modification both of normative and probability projections.

jection. The latter says that the government should aim at a goal irrespective of the likelihood that it may not be fully attained.

In preparing the expenditure projections, our aim was to estimate *probable* developments, including those resulting from the efforts of government to promote a desirable rate of growth. But not all government programs are included that might be considered desirable in the interest of economic growth or of social objectives or that have been recommended by various groups of knowledgeable and responsible experts.[2]

Nevertheless, estimates are presented here that are compatible with the goals of a desirable rate of growth and reasonable price stability, because the government is not likely for long to pursue a policy that would be incompatible with these goals. The kind of federal budget that is in accord with these objectives will depend on activities in the private domestic sector—expenditure and saving by consumers and investment and saving by business—in the state-local government sector, and in international transactions projected for the same period. With respect to these activities outside the federal sector, the projections here are in line with the National Economic Projection Series (NEPS) of the National Planning Association.[3] As federal expenditures were estimated independently of the NEPS projections, the federal budget projections have to be brought into accord with the economic projections by variations in the assumptions for future changes in tax legislation. In the models projecting a relatively small increase in expenditures a larger tax cut has to be assumed during the period covered by the study. For the models showing a larger increase in expenditures a smaller future tax reduction, or none at all, is assumed. Thus, the budget projections of Model II, as they are summarized in Chapter I, are believed compatible with a sustained 4 percent rate of growth implied in the NEPS judgment model. It is a probability model—implying the probability that the government will pursue expenditure and tax

[2] There is a difference between the budget projection in this research project and the program implications of the study by Leonard A. Lecht on *Goals, Priorities, and Dollars* (to be published for the National Planning Association, by the Free Press, early in 1966), which presents cost estimates of the "aspiration goals" that have been recommended by responsible groups, even though it is not believed feasible or probable that all goals can be attained in full within a limited period of time.

[3] The "judgment" model is used here, which does allow for some "slippage" in the pursuit of general economic objectives.

policies in support of economic growth and stability but will operate in a somewhat less than perfect manner in pursuit of these objectives.

Bottom-Up or Top-Down Estimates

Budget-making is always a mixture of from-the-top-down and from-the-bottom-up procedures. The agencies are given guidelines from the Budget Bureau, and then they prepare the individual estimates. The estimates are examined and often revised by the Budget Bureau, which determines the merits of the particular agency proposals in their own right and in the light of a budget total that the Budget Bureau or the President may envisage for the ensuing year.

The same kind of interplay would probably take place if medium- and long-term projections were prepared by the Budget Bureau. The estimation procedure in this study was different, for all estimates had to be prepared by a small private research group. Only through voluntary interviews could general views be obtained, and in no case were specific estimates received from agencies or their subdivisions. Nevertheless, these expenditure estimates were arrived at predominantly through a "from-the-bottom-up" procedure. We started from details and made revisions subsequently in order to assure some consistency among the various functions of the government.

For each function only one estimate was made in detail. This estimate was a projection of existing programs unless new programs were explicitly included. With this estimate as a guide, the aggregates for each function were developed for the different models. This was because we decided to use alternatives for nondefense functions only after the basic estimates had been completed.

One of the principal objectives was to work through the estimates, simulating as closely as possible the actual conditions under which agency officials might be expected to undertake this task. This involved a laborious "build-up" of figures at the same level of detail as in the budget table presenting an "Analysis of New Obligational Authority and Expenditures by Agency" (Part V of the budget document). The study extended to the level of object classification detail based on the tables appearing in the budget appendix. This level of detail was omitted in the final version for reasons of space and also because its inclusion might have given a misleading impression of accuracy. However, this method, taken by itself, proved to have definite shortcomings.

The first is the relative structural inflexibility of estimates derived in this way. The problems presented by new programs and program contractions present a second difficulty, and they are described separately.

Other problems in the "detail method" of making projections include the tendency to overestimate expenditures during the next few years and to underestimate them in the longer-run period, and the difficulty of divorcing oneself from a framework that is already set up. This problem is especially serious for agency budget officers.

The second approach we have used in making our projections is best described as a "top-down" approach. For this, we divided expenditures into their broad functional categories and then projected them within the framework of the expected over-all economic development. Thus, here again projections of GNP and its components, as well as population projections and other economic data, were utilized as a frame for estimating expenditure levels. Further, for Model II, a very rough projection of needs for an evaluation of various additional domestic programs was considered necessary.

It will be seen that the figures derived from these two principal approaches necessarily differ, though the trends emerge clearly enough. Where the differences were great, an adjustment was made toward the one that seemed more reasonable within the framework of the over-all economic projections.

Budget Concepts

The detailed estimates had to take as a point of departure the concepts and classifications given in the official budget document. This required certain adjustments. We had to use estimates for administrative units as building blocks for estimates by broader functions. Also for certain details it was necessary to use estimated requirements for obligational authority and to adjust them to the expenditure base. To the estimates for the agencies were added those for trust accounts, but interfund transfers were eliminated in order to obtain the consolidated cash estimates.

For the summary, we had to choose between expressing our projections in terms of the administrative budget, the consolidated cash statement of federal receipts and payments (hereinafter called the cash budget), and the federal sector of the national income and products account (called the national income budget).

The cash budget was found to be the most useful for the purposes of this study because it is the most comprehensive one. It includes receipts and payments of trust accounts, which are excluded from the conventional administrative budget, and it includes transactions involving existing assets and certain other financial transactions that are excluded from the national income budget. For an economic analysis the national income budget has the advantage that it is presented where feasible on an accrual basis, which measures transactions nearer to the time of their economic impact than do cash payments. The national income budget also fits better into economic projections that are expressed in terms of national income and product accounts. Nevertheless, it was decided to make primary use of the most comprehensive concept—the consolidated cash budget. However, for projections of specific programs and for agency detail projections, estimates in terms of the administrative budget have also been used to make them comparable with those of the base year as recorded in the budget document. For purposes of comparing our budget totals with the national economic projections, we had to translate our cash estimates into national income accounts of the federal sector. This translation posed certain technical difficulties. It became clear that there is a need for better reconciliation between the national income budget on the one hand, and the administrative and cash budgets on the other.

Some of the agency detail can be given more conveniently in terms of the administrative budget. In order to save space the agency details have not been adjusted to a cash basis, except in presenting the budget totals.

None of the three budget concepts reflects government guarantees, loan insurance, or other similar devices for stimulating private or local government investments, except for the actual outlays that are made to cover defaults of insured or guaranteed loans, and these have been negligible in size. These guaranteed and insured loans are estimated for fiscal 1966 at $99.1 billion, or $7.3 billion higher than those estimated for fiscal 1965 and $13 billion higher than in

1964. For a complete evaluation of the impact of government programs on economic development the guarantee and insurance programs should not be neglected.[4] Disregarding these indirect methods of support is especially misleading when activities are shifted from direct loan expenditures to loan guarantees and loan insurance. But in this study no allowance is made in the projections for loan guarantees and insurance or similar devices. Their effect is difficult to measure because some of the loans would undoubtedly have been made even without federal support. Nevertheless, if projections should be made regularly in the future by either a government agency or a private organization, a projection of these activities should be presented at least as an appendix to the budget projections proper.

Payments have not been classified here into current expenditures and capital outlays. The conventional definition of capital outlays as expenditures for durable goods is too narrow for government purposes. It would certainly be desirable to identify outlays for programs that are designed to promote future productivity and economic growth; but for practical reasons such a classification was not attempted in the present study.

The program budget used by the Department of Defense represents a mission-oriented reclassification of the various aspects of the Department's activities. The traditional classification is by appropriation account. Figures for the Defense Department are given under both classifications. Program budgeting will probably spread gradually to other agencies and may in time replace the present system of appropriation accounts.

As for gross and net expenditures, appropriation laws permit certain receipts (fees for services, repayment of loans, sale of assets, and other receipts and reimbursements) to be credited as offsets to expenditures. This permission extends to administrative agencies and trust funds as well as to government-sponsored enterprises.

For the fiscal year 1966, for instance, gross expenditures of the federal government are estimated at $155 billion, or $28 billion more than cash payments to the public and $55 billion more than expenditures in the administrative budget.

It is quite clear that a cash budget is more useful than the con-

[4] George F. Break, *The Economic Impact of Federal Loan Insurance* (National Planning Association, 1961).

ventional budget for purposes of economic analysis. It is less clear whether gross expenditures are also superior to payments in the cash budget. For a detailed analysis it would be better to evaluate the expansionary effect of gross expenditures and then evaluate separately the offsetting effect not only of tax payments but also of payments of fees (for example, for postal services), of receipts of public enterprises, revolving funds, sale of assets, and other reimbursements. For example, the effects of government programs in housing and community development are certainly underestimated here. Measured by the administrative budget they are virtually zero. In the cash budget they are about $700 million. Counting them as gross expenditures, that is at $3.5 billion, gives a more appropriate picture of government activity in this field. However, the fact that the largest part of these expenditures is offset by repayments of loans and sales of assets reduces the budget accounts by the full amount of these receipts but reduces the effect on economic expansion to only a limited extent. Also it should be remembered that government guaranteed and insured loans are not reflected in any of the expenditure estimates—not even gross expenditures. Table 6 gives for the fiscal year 1966 estimated gross expenditures compared with expenditures in the administrative budget and the cash budget.

Following budget practice, the legally permitted offsets have been deducted from the expenditure data used for the projections in this study, even though it is recognized that this method of accounting understates somewhat the true rise of government activities and their effect on the economy.

Time Perspective

The projections have been made on a year-by-year basis in order to reproduce federal procedures as faithfully as possible. However, the study distinguishes among short-term projections, covering the next fiscal year, medium-term projections, covering a period of up to five years, and long-term projections, looking up to ten years ahead.

We have found it essential to review all projections on a continuing basis. During the two-year period of this study many changes occurred in policies and in the economic and political situation that

TABLE 6. Federal Expenditures Proposed for Fiscal 1966 in Terms of the Administrative Budget, Cash Payments to the Public, and Gross Expenditures

(In billions of current dollars)

Item	Administrative budget expenditures	Cash payments to public	Gross expenditures
National defense	51.6	52.5	54.2
International affairs	4.0	4.2	5.4
Space research and technology	5.1	5.1	5.1
Agriculture and agricultural resources	3.9	4.1	15.8
Natural resources	2.7	2.9	3.2
Commerce and transportation	2.8	6.5	12.3
Housing and community development	a	0.7	3.5
Health, labor, and welfare	8.3	34.1	33.6
Education	2.7	2.6	2.7
Veterans benefits and services	4.6	5.1	6.8
Interest	11.6	8.8	9.5
General government	2.5	2.4	2.4
Allowance for Appalachia	0.1	0.1 ⎫	
Allowance for contingencies	0.4	0.4 ⎬	0.5
Adjustments	−0.6	−2.0 ⎭	
Total	99.7	127.4	155.0

ᵃ Less than $50 million.

called for revisions. While on a long-term, over-all basis such changes may not loom large, they are important for the next year and several years ahead. When projections are prepared within the federal government on a regular schedule, it is essential that they be kept up to date on a continuing basis.

Short-Term Projections

Under the present system, the preparation of estimates for federal budget expenditures begins as long as eighteen months before the beginning of the relevant fiscal year. Until some years ago, the budget estimates were based entirely on short-term economic forecasts of gross national product, personal income, payrolls, profits, and the consumption of taxable products. This means, in effect, that short-term economic assumptions are used to estimate expenditures as long as thirty months ahead. For revenue estimates, the time period is shorter because they do not involve the same time-consuming agency hearings prior to the budget formulation. This method has always run into difficulties whenever economists have believed that a recession might occur during the budget period. This would mean lower revenues and possibly even higher expenditures, for example, for payments from the unemployment trust funds. Under various administrations overly optimistic economic forecasts have been used as a basis for preparing the budget in order to reduce the dilemma for the President of either showing a politically embarrassing large deficit or paring down proposals for expenditures that are believed desirable, especially if a recession appears imminent. Furthermore, if an administration predicts the likelihood of a recession, would it not then also be expected to propose, or to take, timely action to forestall such an event? Forecasting the likelihood of a recession could imply that antirecession measures would not be adopted or would not succeed. A corresponding dilemma would arise if inflation were predicted.

From this point of view, it is preferable to base the budget proposals on the assumption of a "normal" rate of growth, rather than on a prediction. In the budget message, it can then be pointed out what the effect on the budget would be of either a threatening inflation or a recession.

Actually in recent years the federal budget proposals have moved in the direction of a desired (rather than a probable) course of economic developments. However, these economic assumptions have been announced, or at least interpreted, as actual forecasts. We propose that the budget preparation be clearly based on a realistic approximation to a full employment economy and on the assumption that the government will adopt needed measures to promote economic growth and stability. Then in the budget message and the economic report of the President the most likely course of the economy could be contrasted with the assumptions, and additional corrective policies could be proposed.

Medium- and Long-Term Projections

For the medium-term projections, for two to five years in the future, estimates could be made in the same detail as in Part V of the budget document, "The Federal Program by Agency." Estimates for the broad functional classifications will also be needed, of course. Cyclical changes cannot readily be built into medium- and longer-range budget projections with any degree of accuracy.

For long-term projections, for a period of more than five years ahead, projections of the major tax sources and expenditures at a level of detail corresponding to the principal functional budget classifications are quite feasible. However, unless they are strictly limited to broad outlines, budget projections are not really meaningful for periods of more than a decade ahead.

With respect to the time perspective, there is a methodological problem similar to that noticed with respect to "from-the-top-down" or "from-the-bottom-up" procedure. For longer-range projections, either estimates can be developed on a year-by-year basis (forward projecting), or an estimate can be made for the terminal year of a period and then the intervening years can be estimated by backward interpolation. While both methods have their uses, it was considered better for this study to make year-by-year estimates in the first instance. In fact "built-up" estimates can be made only in this manner. This approach is thorough, but it involves a lot of detail work. For example, figures for a number of years prior to the base year have to be reviewed for most programs, since in practice, agency budget officers tend to regard the previous year's figures as a starting point when preparing requests for agency expenditures for the ensuing year. The year-by-year approach on a detail basis has yielded valuable clues concerning the problems and pitfalls inherent in this method. To a considerable extent, these are similar to the problems already mentioned in describing the "built-up" approach. To counteract these tendencies, results were continuously correlated with projections of the growth of GNP, its component parts, and other over-all economic data, including the growth and age distribution of the population where this was deemed appropriate. In every instance results were also checked for reasonableness and consistency with estimates made for one in-betweeen year (fiscal 1968) and the terminal benchmark year (fiscal 1973), the intervening years being estimated by backward interpolation. Differences resulting from the application of the two methods were reconciled in the light of established trend lines (where these existed) and of reasonableness.

Model I and Model II Assumptions

The differences between Model I and Model II projections have been explained in Chapter I. The two models should not be regarded as alternatives; they mark two different steps in the projection process. First, future expenditures under existing and officially proposed programs were estimated, which gave Model I expenditures and, correspondingly, revenues. Then were added programs or program changes that are already under discussion and are likely to be considered for official recommendation during the period covered in the study. There is no assurance that all such changes that are likely to be adopted have been taken into account or that the time needed to move such changes from the informal discussion phase to the action phase has been correctly estimated. Therefore, it is important that such long-range projections be revised yearly and that the estimates in this study be regarded more as illustrations of a problem than as definitive forecasts.

The work on this study extended over a period in which several federal budgets were presented. A shift in emphasis concerning a number of policies and proposals occurred more than once, but by no means to the same extent in every budget message. This has obviously entailed considerable reworking of the study, and the problem will undoubtedly be present in every budget, with varying degrees of urgency. An annual revision of the longer-term projections will thus be needed.

The problem of how to treat newly emerging needs and entirely new programs presents many difficulties. In some cases, the best solution may lie in setting aside specific reserves for "contingencies" on an agency and a functional level. In a number of areas, responsible committees of experts have explored the need for new programs.[5] Where it was possible, the estimates in this study were based on such reports. But, to repeat, the inclusion of new programs does not necessarily mean that they are recommended.

[5] For example, for oceanography, *A National Ocean Program*, Report of the National Security Industrial Association Ad Hoc Committee on Ocean Science and Technology (March 1964); and *Oceanography, 1960-70*, Report of the Committee on Oceanography, National Academy of Sciences–National Research Council (1959).

Another difficulty faced in building up projections from agency estimates lies in deciding under which agency a new program should be placed. While in some cases the answer is fairly obvious, in others it seemed best to leave this question open. Fortunately the same difficulty does not arise in making estimates by function.

Method of Estimating Revenues

On the revenue side, tax yields were estimated, considering the size of the GNP and its component parts, as described in the assumptions.

No tax changes other than those contained in the budget message of January 1965 (including the excise tax cut and the social security tax changes incorporated in present and proposed legislation) have been spelled out in detail. Even though no specific estimates of additional future tax reductions have been presented, the models imply future tax reductions of various sizes and timing. They will be feasible and needed earlier and to a larger extent in Models I and II-A than in II-B. The timing and size of needed future tax reductions depend not only on the size and character of federal expenditures but also on the development of state and local government finances and on outlays and saving in the private sector. Only within the frame of a detailed projection of the major elements in the national economic accounts can the size and timing of future tax reductions be discussed. This could not be done within the scope of the present study.

Price Indexes and Varying Rates of Growth

The view has been advanced that assuming various rates of growth in any set of models requires also the assumption of differential price increases. Thus, for example, a 5 percent growth rate (after reasonably full employment is reached) is said to put more pressure on prices, and particularly on the wage and salary components of the index, than does a 3 percent growth rate, which puts less strain on available resources, particularly manpower resources. This point of view is most often advanced by those who feel that there cannot be "full employment growth" without causing price increases throughout the economy. In practice the relationship is much more complex, and the answer may be found only in a thorough analysis of what makes for differential productivity gains in an economy, and the influence of such gains on wages, prices, and aggregate demand. Studies of a number of countries experiencing various rates of growth raise some doubt about a close statistical relationship between the rate of growth and of price rises. In a number of countries a fairly stable price level and rapid economic growth have occurred simultaneously; other countries have low economic growth under inflationary conditions; and often the same country may react differently to these factors at different times. No statement about a probable future relationship between the rate of growth and price increases can be made without specific assumptions about policies with respect to prices and wages.

We have not tried to project future price development. We have used two price assumptions which may be regarded as two different measurements of approximate price stability. One method, called projections in "constant prices," uses as a base the level of the GNP price deflator for the average of the four quarters of fiscal 1963 and expresses projected expenditures and revenues as if these price indexes were to remain at the same level. Another method, called projections in "current dollars," assumes a small rise in the price indexes. We have assumed for most of our projections an annual rise of 1.5 percent.[6] A price index measures the price of an identical good or service at two periods of time. When the quality of goods or services rises, the statistician attributes a portion of the price rise to the factor of quality improvement. There is reason to assume that many improvements in quality, particularly those achieved through technological advance, escape the measurement and that at least part of an increase in the price index reflects quality improvements. Therefore, some slight increase in price indexes may not be incompatible with approximate real price stability.[7]

Thus, the assumed increase in "current prices" of 1.5 percent a year should not be regarded as an actual prediction of price development. These estimates in "current prices" are certainly more

[6] Only for the "slow-growth" Model I, a 1.3 percent annual price rise has been assumed. It should be remembered, however, that cost- and price-raising factors need not be absent in an economy of slow growth or stagnation.

[7] There is, of course, also the possibility of quality deterioration. However, considering the fact that new products cannot be properly evaluated in comparison with a time when they did not exist, it is very likely that statistically quality improvements which have not been accounted for outweigh the cases of quality deterioration.

realistic than those in "constant prices." Therefore, the latter have been used only in summary tables mainly in order to facilitate comparison of the projections in this study with those in other studies, which are often expressed in statistically "constant" prices.

Productivity in Government

According to Department of Commerce estimates, prices applicable to the government sector of the national economic accounts have been rising more than prices applicable to other sectors. This is due almost wholly to the fact that the Department of Commerce interprets an increase of 5 percent in the salary of a government employee from one year to the next as a 5 percent increase in the price of the employee's service "bought" by the government. In contrast, if the wage or salary of a worker in private employment increases by 5 percent, this is interpreted as an increase in the cost of the service of 2 percent, while 3 percent is allocated as the employee's participation in the increase in productivity of the economy. The official statistics, in other words, assume no increase in productivity in government service because there is no general measurement available of productivity in government.[8]

We cannot follow this reasoning. It has been the government's policy that at least a part of each salary increase must be absorbed by increased productivity. Most of the managerial and technological advances adopted in private offices are also used in government. It is agreed that a statistical measurement of productivity in government is not available because most of the "output" of government services does not lend itself to quantitative measurement. Nevertheless, it is likely that if an increase in productivity similar to that for private activities is assumed for government services, the error is smaller than if it is assumed that there is no productivity advance in government.

Therefore, our projections for the federal sector assume the same 3 percent a year increase in productivity that has been assumed for the private sector. This means that assumed salary increases of 3 percent a year are not regarded as implying a price increase in the constant-dollar model, while the current-dollar model

[8] The U. S. Bureau of the Budget study published in 1964, *Measuring Productivity of Federal Government Organizations*, refers to only a few samples.

TABLE 7. Price Deflators: Total Gross National Product and Federal Government Sector

(1954=100)

Calendar years	Total GNP	Federal government purchases of goods and services				
		Total		Compensation for employee services		Purchases of goods and other services[b]
		Unadjusted	Adjusted[a]	Unadjusted	Adjusted[a]	
1954	100.0	100.0	100.0	100.0	100.0	100.0
1955	101.2	104.1	102.9	107.3	104.2	102.0
1956	104.6	109.7	107.0	113.1	106.6	107.3
1957	108.4	114.9	111.0	118.1	108.1	112.9
1958	110.8	118.3	112.6	129.5	115.0	111.1
1959	112.6	122.2	115.0	134.5	116.0	114.3
1960	114.2	125.5	116.2	139.2	116.6	116.0
1961	115.8	128.0	117.2	143.7	116.8	117.5
1962	116.7	127.2	115.7	143.8	113.5	117.0
1963	118.5	130.2	116.4	151.2	115.9	116.8
1964[c]	120.7	136.0	118.9	162.9	121.2	117.3

Source: The unadjusted series on compensation for employee services and the weights of compensation for employee services in the total are from unpublished Department of Commerce sources.

[a] Adjusted for 3 percent annual productivity increase deducted from employee compensation component.

[b] All goods and services except employee services.

[c] Preliminary figures.

assumes annual salary increases of 4.5 percent—of which 1.5 percent is treated as a price increase.[9] The results, given in Table 7, show strikingly that after this adjustment there is no significant difference between the price behavior of federal purchases of goods and services and that of the over-all GNP deflator.[10] Separate treatment of the federal component of this deflator, therefore, would not be justified.[11]

[9] For Model I estimates, the assumed price increase is 1.3 percent a year.

[10] However, no changes have been made in the historical figures, since this might create confusion because of a discrepancy between our figures and the official data. Moreover, for past periods (before office automation), it appears more reasonable to assume that productivity gains of federal employees lagged behind those for the entire private sector.

[11] We wish to make it clear that differences between our method and that used by the Department of Commerce in the treatment of productivity in the government sector would not affect any figures expressed in *current* dollars. Only constant-dollar figures would differ.

CHAPTER IV

Problems in Projecting Federal Budgets

THIS CHAPTER CONSIDERS some of the special problems that arise in projecting federal budgets, such as those involved in predicting the future course of federal-state-local fiscal relations, of the government-business relationship, and of the ratio of the federal budget to an increasing gross national product. It also considers the staffing needs of the Budget Bureau if the projections are to be undertaken on a regular basis and some of the political problems involved.

Federal-State-Local Fiscal Relations

In the past fifty years federal-state-local fiscal relationships have undergone drastic changes. Before World War I, the federal government accounted for 30 percent of total government cash expenditures. In 1952 the percentage had increased to 72 percent (including federal grants) and declined to 64 percent by the fiscal year 1963. The main contributing factors were the large increases in federal defense expenditures, expenditures resulting from previous wars, and the federal old age and survivors' social insurance system.

However, excluding defense and international expenditures and expenditures resulting from previous wars, the federal government share doubled temporarily during the depression but declined after World War II. During the last decade these domestic nondefense federal expenditures have shown a rising trend, as Table 8 shows.[1]

TABLE 8. Domestic Nondefense Expenditures of Federal, State, and Local Governments, Selected Years, 1902–63[a]

Fiscal Years	Totals (In billions of current dollars)	Federal expenditures as a percentage of federal, state, and local government expenditures	
		Including intergovernmental transfers	Excluding intergovernmental transfers
1902	1,325	17.9%	17.4%
1913	2,765	18.8	18.4
1927	9,261	17.0	15.7
1936	13,410	43.4	36.6
1953	48,898	38.5	32.6
1963	119,828	43.9	36.8

Sources: U. S. Bureau of the Census, *The U. S. Census of Governments*, "Historical Statistics on Governmental Finances and Employment," Vol. VI, No. 4 (1964); U. S. Bureau of the Census, *Governmental Finances in 1963* (November 1964).

[a] See note 1 to the text for an explanation of the data used.

Over the next decade federal expenditures for defense and defense-related programs may level off or decline while the greatest increase may occur in programs that traditionally belong to local jurisdictions, such as education, urban development and mass transportation, police protection, and so on. In contrast, federal revenues, particularly from income and profits taxes, will in general rise faster in response to economic growth than will local tax receipts. This may lead to a situation where federal income taxes could be reduced periodically to prevent a "fiscal drag" while local tax rates

[1] U. S. Bureau of the Census data were used both in the paragraph above and in Table 8 because only these historical data for both the federal and state-local governments were available on a comparable basis. The concepts used include trust fund expenditures, which are significant in this relationship. For the table, domestic nondefense expenditures were defined to include for the federal government total expenditures less the functional categories of national defense and international affairs, interest on the general debt, and veterans' services not elsewhere classified; and for state-local government, the total expenditures.

are continuously raised. Alternatives are a continued rise in federal grants-in-aid to state and local programs or some tax-sharing arrangement between the federal government and state and local governments.

The projections in all models assume a very substantial increase in federal grant-in-aid programs. Table 9 shows grants-in-aid as a share of federal expenditures in 1953 and 1963 and the projections under various models for 1973. In addition, as was pointed out in Chapter I, before 1973 a situation is likely to arise calling for either another cut in federal tax rates or some tax-sharing arrangement. The latter alternative would make it possible for state and local governments to improve their services without increasing tax rates. Specific consideration of these and other alternatives of the future federal-state-local financial relationships was believed to be outside the scope of the present study. Nevertheless, it should be emphasized that it will become increasingly necessary to consider the national tax system (including state and local taxes and also social security taxes) as an interrelated whole.

TABLE 9. Model I and Model II: Grants-in-Aid as a Percentage of Federal Expenditures, National Income Budget, Fiscal Years, 1953, 1963, 1966, and 1973

Item	1953	1963	1966	1973
Actual grants-in-aid	3.7	7.4		
Proposed grants-in-aid			10.2	
Projected grants-in-aid in:				
Model I				14.1
Model II-A1				14.4
Model II-A2				15.1
Model II-B				17.0

Government-Business Relationship

The projections in this study are based on the assumption that the government will take over only functions that cannot or cannot adequately be performed by private enterprise. It is not always easy, however, to decide where the line of demarcation should be drawn between government activity and private enterprise. In this respect, the last few decades have brought important innovations.

Gone are the times when government provided only clearly defined administrative, protective, and judicial services and private enterprise provided all production and distribution of goods and other services (if such times really ever existed).

There were the "emergency" activities of the federal government during the depression of the thirties, which brought about, for example, the electrification of certain private railroads. Another example is provided by the federal guarantees, insurance programs, and in some cases purchases of mortgages, which have helped in the construction and purchase of about 28 percent of all privately owned and privately built homes in this country since the inception of these programs. Federal support of home financing has broadened into the fields of slum clearance, urban renewal, and mass transportation, which have required cooperation among the federal government, local governments, and private enterprise, and sometimes also nonprofit private organizations.

The World War II and Korean War periods again saw new developments of government-business cooperation in government-owned, but privately operated, factories for defense production. Postwar weapons and space technology made the federal government the main financial source for research and development in the United States. The government has been financing most of the research and development costs for the peacetime use of atomic energy and of a by-product (isotopes) of greatest usefulness for medical, agricultural, and industrial purposes. New forms of government-business relationships have been tried in this field too.

During the fiscal year 1964, the federal government provided more than $15 billion for all kinds of research and development— about two-thirds of all funds devoted to this purpose in the United States during this period. This not only contributed to the development of new industries, like electronics and space equipment, but affected indirectly the whole level of technological sophistication of American industry. Much of the government-financed research for government purposes is carried out under contract by private enterprise and private research organizations. Going even further, the Communications Satellite Corporation (COMSAT) represents a new departure, a semiprivate, semipublic organization created for the commercial utilization of space communication facilities on an international scale.

It is indeed difficult to foresee what the future of this government-business relationship is likely to be and what impact it may
have on future budgets. There are now pending new developments
in such fields as the desalinization of brackish or sea water, water and
air pollution, weather control, further developments in space exploration, the farming and mining of the oceans, new technologies in
rapid ground transportation, supersonic air transportation, new research efforts in such areas as high-energy physics, astronomy, and
so on. These are examples of fields in which expenses and risks for
research and development exceed what private enterprise and aca-
demic and other nonprofit research organizations are able or willing
to undertake without some kind of government support. If the federal government participates in further development in these fields,
this could add large expenditures to federal budgets. Alternatively,
the federal government might furnish indirect support, possibly in
the form of subsidies or loan guarantees, which would mobilize private funds as well and use private management and talent as far as
possible, with much smaller additions to the budget.

Actually the projections here assume that, where it appears feasible and efficient, the government will support private efforts rather
than perform these quasi-commercial functions itself. Therefore,
only limited amounts have been included in Model II budgets for
these purposes. The impact of government action, however, is not
fully measured by the impact of the expenditures directly included
in the budgets.

The Federal Budget and GNP

As was stated in Chapter I, the Model II projections anticipate
in only one of the alternative combinations a small increase in the
relationship of federal spending to the growing GNP (Model II-B).
Even in that particular case, the ratio would be below that for fiscal
1963. In all other combinations the share of the federal sector declines somewhat, particularly in the case where a reduction in defense expenditures is assumed (Model II-A2). Projected revenues
were cut by the reduction in excise taxes to the extent proposed by
the President in his budget message (and therefore included in
Models I and II). In Model II-A further substantial tax cuts or the

sharing of federal revenue with state-local governments are implicitly assumed to become effective before the end of the period under consideration. Thus, the federal government would support economic growth in the coming decade both by an increase in programs and by some further tax reduction. The models imply that for the next decade the expansion in programs will probably make a greater contribution to economic growth than will tax reduction. Nevertheless, future policy could emphasize either program expansion or tax reduction. In order to demonstrate these possibilities, alternative projections are presented here, assuming more or less rapid program expansion, associated with little or substantial further tax cuts, respectively.

An increase in programs designed to combat poverty would open up new mass markets and thereby have an impact on business opportunities. A related increase in educational and training programs would help to meet the skill requirements of modern technology. The increase in programs of a developmental character (urban renewal, transportation, new technologies) would raise the horizon for new private investment and thereby affect the development of the nation's economic potential (the "leverage effect" of government programs).

Increases in such programs do not merely affect economic growth directly. They could be designed to maintain a balance, in combination with tax reductions, between the increase in the economic potential and the increase in aggregate purchasing power.

Several critical questions may be asked about the economic aspects of these projections.

1. What about economic fluctuations? It is believed that the Model II projections are in accord with the requirements of a reasonable rate of sustained economic growth. A steadfast policy in support of economic growth reduces the likelihood of severe recessions. Nevertheless, it would be utopian to expect that policies in support of steady growth will always be perfect and fully successful. Therefore, it is reasonable to expect that fluctuations will occur at least in the rate of growth and possibly at times even in the level of activities. For this contingency, anticyclical monetary and fiscal policies should be held in readiness. This topic was, however, out-

side the scope of the present study. As was mentioned above, it is for this reason that the projections are not to be regarded as predictions for any specific year (which may turn out to be a recession year) but rather as benchmarks on a trendline.

2. Some believe that in this age of technological development and urbanization, government responsibilities are bound to increase in both absolute and relative terms, and that this will be reflected in a rising ratio of the budget to GNP. This is not assumed in our study.

We are dealing only with the federal budget. As was mentioned above, the increase in expenditures for nondefense activities has been larger at the state-local level than at the federal level. Some of the growing responsibilities of the federal government, however, are not fully reflected in the federal budget. There are indirect ways in which the government contributes to economic growth and welfare. Furthermore, there is a question about the continuing validity of the thesis (first pronounced 75 years ago) that the share of government is bound to rise along with increased industrialization and urbanization.[2] While certain government responsibilities rise with increasing abundance, others may decline.

3. Our budget projections do not provide for any systematic repayment of the national debt, but rather envisage the possibility of some further increase in the debt. Would this not result in continuing inflationary tendencies?

Debt-financed deficits are undesirable if they contribute to excessive demand and price inflation. Of a different nature, however, are deficits which, in combination with appropriate monetary policies, can prevent an otherwise likely deflation and economic contraction. A growing economy requires a broadening financial structure. This will be brought about primarily by an expanding private capital base. With the relative importance of the public sector, steady economic growth without some increase in the public debt (federal or state-local) is hardly conceivable. An alternative to a broadening of the financial superstructure of the economy would be a steady price decline. This is not a realistic alternative, however, except under conditions of a prolonged economic depression. When

[2] Adolph Wagner, *Finanzwissenschaft*, 4 vols. (Leipzig, 1877-1901); Vol. I, 3rd ed., 1883; Vols. II-III, 2nd ed., 1880-1912.

the government debt increases because of federal spending to support economic growth, the relationship of the debt to GNP does not rise. It is not the absolute amount of the national debt that is important for an evaluation of the "debt burden," but rather the relationship of the debt and the debt service to GNP and taxable incomes. This ratio has been steadily declining and, according to our projections, will continue to decline. Actually the ratio of the federal debt to GNP declined during the decade from the end of 1954 to 1964 from 75 percent to 51.7 percent. Under our projections it would decline further to about 40 percent by 1973.

In contrast to a growth-supporting increase in the national debt, recession deficits are caused by declining taxable incomes and profits and increasing payments for unemployment and social assistance benefits. They lead to an increase in the debt in relation to a stagnant or declining GNP and result in an increase in the real burden of the debt.

The Model II projections are based on the assumption that the relationship between government payments and receipts will be adjusted to fit into the pattern of balanced economic growth without causing either inflationary excess demand or a purchasing power deficiency in relation to the economic potential.

In the Model II projections a steady small increase in prices (1.5 percent a year) is assumed as measured by the available price indexes. This is not meant as a forecast but really as a stable price assumption, taking into account that price indexes do not make adequate allowances for quality improvements. It may well be that prices will at times rise by more than 1.5 percent during the coming years. A larger price rise in the United States, however, is more likely to be initiated by the operation of the wage-price or price-wage spiral than by a limited increase in the national debt.

Administrative Requirements

An adequate staff is needed if budget projections are to become a regular responsibility of the federal government. The projections presented in this study were prepared by a small staff of a private research organization with no authority to ask the several government agencies to prepare estimates for their fields of responsibility. Numerous interviews were held with agency officials and with Budget Bureau personnel. They were very helpful. However, in no case were estimates obtained from government agencies which could be used directly for our own estimates.

On the basis of our study it seems certain that with an adequate staff the Budget Bureau could prepare intermediate- and long-term budget projections as a regular routine function. They should be revised periodically. It was necessary, even within the relatively short lifetime of this project, to revise earlier estimates to a considerable extent. For example, some estimates had to be moved from Model II to Model I after President Johnson's messages of January 1965.

Some observations were made in the course of this study which should be of value for future work:

At the working level of making projections, it is difficult to achieve harmony between projections built from the ground up on a detailed agency basis, and less detailed projections based on a functional program approach.

In the agency interviews, a recurring pattern appeared. Increases in expenditures were estimated for the one or two years following the next budget year, then a leveling off, and a slight but persistent decline after the five-year level. Psychologically the tendency can be explained by the fact that the agency budget for the ensuing budget period had probably been cut back by the Bureau of the Budget and the Congress below the level the agency thought desirable, and this had resulted in an accumulation of programs regarded as worthwhile for possibly as long as two or three years ahead. After that period, however, it becomes difficult to treat future needs imaginatively within an agency framework, and it is in this context that functional estimates based on calculations worked out from the top down furnish a useful check.

When it comes to the estimates of new programs or program contraction, the agencies are often not able (or inclined) to provide the needed information.[3] Here the Budget Bureau would have to play a major role.[4] This applies particularly to the question of dis-

[3] For a discussion of special problems pertaining to new programs, see pp. 45-46.

[4] The senior author cannot refrain from recording the following anecdote. In 1944, when he was assigned the task of projecting a postwar federal budget, he had an interview with a well-known admiral who was assigned to work on plans

continuing or cutting back existing programs because at the agency level it is never easy to visualize that any of them may be dispensable.

Nevertheless, it is very important that agency heads be asked to consider intermediate- and long-term budget requirements in their fields. Quite apart from the value of obtaining this information, it is of considerable educational value if the heads of the agencies and bureaus are forced to look at their programs in a longer time perspective.

Adequate staffing arrangements are required for this work, both at the agency level and in the Budget Bureau. The need is obviously most pressing at the agency level, particularly since it seems undesirable that personnel engaged on current agency problems should be too deeply involved in future projections in any major role. There are few persons trained to estimate agency programs for a number of years ahead in a responsible fashion and yet imaginatively. It may be advisable to coordinate their training with the Bureau of the Budget.

There will also be additional staff requirements in the Bureau of the Budget. The Bureau already has a number of qualified persons with experience in this field who could form the nucleus of any group dealing with budget projections. However, these persons are usually swamped with current work, and an increase in personnel capable of performing projections work and of working well with agency personnel would be highly desirable.

Political Considerations

Some skeptics, while conceding that meaningful budget projections can be made, say that it would not be desirable to have longer-term projections prepared and published by the government itself. Actually the federal government has been preparing budget projections for internal purposes but has rarely approved their pub-

---

for a postwar Navy. When asked about the Navy's thinking about the required size of annual expenditures for a postwar Navy under general assumptions which were given to him, the only answer that could be obtained from the admiral was "First you have to tell me what total defense expenditures will be. Then I can answer your question for the Navy. The Navy always requires at least one-third of the expenditures for the total defense establishment."

lication.[5] For one thing, it is feared that estimates concerning future years would be interpreted as definite decisions. If the estimates are done in a spirit of boldness, they may raise premature controversy. If they are done with caution and restraint, they may bind the hands of the administration for future action. And there is a general and understandable tendency in government not to show its hand earlier than is absolutely necessary. There is also sometimes the fear that showing the full future budget impact of programs under consideration may reduce congressional willingness to authorize them.

These arguments cannot easily be dismissed. But they are not necessarily conclusive. By presenting alternative projections, based on existing legislation and policy recommendations, on the one hand, and on possible future changes, on the other, the difference between programs that are officially recommended and those that are under consideration for future determination can be clearly demonstrated. Estimates for programs that are under debate will contribute toward a better informed consideration of such programs. Nevertheless, as was mentioned above (pages 16-17), some time may be needed until this difference between recommended and considered programs and policies is fully understood. This difficulty, real as it is, should not represent an immovable obstacle to the preparation and eventual publication of longer-term projections by the government.

One reason why the executive branch should not only prepare but also publish intermediate- and long-term projections is that such projections should be available to Congress. They are needed for a more meaningful examination of budgets for the ensuing year by the appropriations committees, for a better-informed consideration of pending tax legislation by the House Ways and Means and the Senate Finance Committees, and especially for the appraisal of the economic outlook by the Joint Economic Committee of Congress. The latter has been suggested as the most logical body to examine interrelated budget and economic projections (without going into details of appropriations or tax legislation) and to transmit the result of its study to the legislative committees. This would probably be preferable to the revival of the Joint Budget Committee, whose

[5] See pp. 2-3, especially note 8.

experiences were not very encouraging.[6] It is recognized that a great deal of educational work may be necessary before the American public will understand the proper role and the advantages of projections of federal receipts and expenditures for a longer period ahead.

It would be the task of private research organizations to pave the way for a better understanding of the issues involved by focusing attention on them and by familiarizing the public with the whole concept of these projections.

It is also important that the fullest amount of intelligent public discussion be stimulated by the publication of alternative projections from government and private sources.

[6] For a more detailed discussion, see Gerhard Colm, *The Federal Budget and the National Economy*, Planning Pamphlet No. 90 (National Planning Association, 1955), pp. 64 ff.

PART TWO

Projections of Federal
Revenues and Expenditures

CHAPTER V

Projections of
Federal Receipts

PROJECTIONS OF FEDERAL revenues depend on many variables, most of which are beyond the scope of this study. They include such variables as private investment, personal consumption expenditures, and state and local government spending. While assumptions have been made concerning all of them (see Appendix Table A-1), the study has not been concerned with their derivation in detail.

For this reason, our revenue figures are only illustrative. This is true particularly of Model II-A, and to a lesser extent also of Model I, because the attainment of the revenue figures shown will depend on the adoption of a number of other measures, as is outlined in the discussion of each model below.

Tax Revenues and the Rate of Economic Growth

The most important single determinant in any projection of federal revenues is the rate of economic growth that is assumed for the period under consideration. Details of the assumptions made here for our various models regarding growth rates are given in Chapter

I. Except for a few minor adjustments, which are described under the appropriate tax involved, no changes in legislation affecting revenues have been assumed beyond the excise tax cuts proposed by the administration in the January 1965 budget message.

The crucial importance of the rate of growth for all revenue estimates can be illustrated by the following example. At the present time (the first quarter of 1965) the GNP is probably about $20-$25 billion below the level of reasonably full employment (not more than 4 percent unemployment). Merely reaching this level of employment would require an increase in economic activities that would raise federal revenues by at least $5 billion, since profits would be especially strong in such a recovery.

Once that level of employment is attained, every $10 billion of increase in GNP will result in an increase in federal tax revenues of about $2 billion, without any change in tax legislation. After reaching the "reasonably full employment level" the assumed continuing rate of growth of 4 percent annually in real terms implies an increase in revenues in excess of $8 billion annually. In turn, the fact that the level of taxation in relation to the level of expenditures is itself a very important determinant of the rate of economic growth is one of the main reasons why budget projections in the framework of economic projections are a necessity for fiscal and economic planning. In this chapter account is taken of the influence of economic growth on tax revenue. The effect of expenditures and revenues on economic growth has been discussed in Chapters I and II.

Over-all Revenue Projections

Even a brief look at the revenue projections summarized in Table 10 confirms the fact that economic growth is the main determinant of future revenue. Under the by no means extravagant assumptions for economic growth, federal receipts in Models II-A and II-B (according to the consolidated cash budget) would increase by 18 percent over a two-year period to 1968, and by about 60 percent by 1973—assuming no changes in present tax legislation. This increase would give an opportunity for an increase in needed federal programs, a transfer of revenue to state and local governments, a reduction in tax rates, or some combination of the three.

It is assumed in Model II-B that pressure for making up deficiencies in government programs is so strong that the increase in revenue would be used largely for financing an increase in expenditures on the federal or state-local level primarily through considerably increased grants-in-aid to the states and increases in transfer payments. In addition, the substantial increases in grants-in-aid projected in Model II-B would enable state and local governments to keep local taxation well below levels that would otherwise be necessary. This would mean an effective further measure of tax relief to individuals and corporations.

By contrast, in Model II-A the choice is deliberately left open whether the excess of revenues over expenditures is to be used for periodic federal tax reductions or for benefiting state and local governments by tax sharing arrangements or a system of unconditional grants. Conceivably a combination of all three methods could be used, particularly if some arms reduction should prove feasible. It should be repeated here that the revenue estimates made under the assumption of present or presently proposed (as of January 1965) tax rates should be regarded only as a basis from which the feasibility of, and need for, future tax reduction could be considered. This applies especially to Model II-A. Without some further measures on the tax side the assumed rate of growth could not be expected to develop.

Similar considerations apply to Model I, for which a lower rate of growth has been assumed. Tax revenues have been worked out accordingly. In the consolidated cash budget they will increase (from 1966) by less than 12 percent by 1968 and by 42 percent by 1973. However, in this case, too, a reduction in taxes or adoption of one of the other measures described may be necessary, particularly for 1970 and subsequent years, in order to achieve even the more limited objectives assumed for this model.

Projections by Major Tax Sources

The revenue estimates have been worked out in accordance with the projected assumptions described in Chapter I (pages 3-7). Within this framework, estimates for the various major sources of receipts have been worked out for the period 1967-73 for the consolidated cash budget. Over-all revenue projections have also been

TABLE 10. Model I and Model II: Federal Receipts in Administrative Budget, Cash Budget, and National Income Accounts, 1963, 1966, 1968, and 1973[a]

(In billions of current dollars for fiscal years)

Item	Actual 1963	Proposed 1966	Projected 1968			Projected 1973		
			Model I[b]	Model II-A[b]	Model II-B	Model I[b]	Model II-A[b]	Model II-B
Gross national product	568.0	681.5	739.5	771.0	771.0	921.5	1,007.5	1,007.5
Personal income	452.1	538.5	586.5	604.5	604.5	740.0	786.0	786.0
Corporate profits	48.6	66.0	67.5	76.1	76.1	73.5	99.5	99.5
Federal Receipts—Administrative Budget and Cash Budget								
Individual income tax	47.6	48.2	(52.7)	(56.0)	56.0	(69.0)	(76.2)	76.2
Corporate profits tax	21.6	27.6	(28.9)	(31.9)	31.9	(32.0)	(40.9)	40.9
Excise taxes	9.9	9.8	(10.5)	(11.3)	11.3	(14.0)	(16.0)	16.0
Estate and gift taxes	2.2	3.2	(3.4)	(4.0)	4.0	(3.9)	(6.0)	6.0
Customs	1.2	1.5	(1.7)	(1.8)	1.8	(2.2)	(2.6)	2.6
Other	3.9	4.1	(3.7)	(3.7)	3.7	(4.2)	(4.5)	4.5
Total receipts, administrative budget	86.4	94.4	(100.9)	(108.7)	108.7	(125.3)	(146.2)	146.2

Employment taxes	14.9	18.7	(25.3)	(26.0)	26.0	(33.8)	(36.7)	36.9
Deposits by states (unemployment insurance)	3.0	2.9	(3.2)	(3.0)	3.0	(5.0)	(4.0)	4.0
Gasoline and other highway excises	3.3	4.0	(4.4)	(4.4)	4.4	(5.4)	(5.4)	6.5
Other, less interfund transactions	6.5	8.1	(8.8)	(9.0)	9.0	(10.7)	(11.1)	11.1
Less: intergovernment transactions	−4.3	−4.5	(−4.7)	(−4.7)	−4.7	(−5.0)	(−5.0)	−5.0
Total, net trust fund receipts	23.4	29.1	(37.0)	(37.7)	37.7	(49.9)	(52.2)	53.5
Total receipts, cash budget	109.7	123.5	(137.9)	(146.4)	146.4	(175.2)	(198.4)	199.7
Total receipts as a percentage of GNP	19.3	18.1	(18.6)	(19.0)	19.0	(19.0)	(19.7)	19.8

Federal Receipts—National Income Accounts

Personal tax and nontax receipts	50.1	52.2	(57.0)	(61.0)	61.0	(74.0)	(83.3)	83.3
Corporate profits tax accruals	22.1	24.7	(28.2)	(31.0)	31.0	(31.5)	(40.9)	40.9
Indirect business tax and nontax accruals	15.2	16.1	(17.3)	(18.5)	18.5	(23.0)	(25.5)	26.7
Contributions for social insurance	22.1	28.0	(33.5)	(34.0)	34.0	(45.5)	(47.3)	47.6
Total, national income accounts	109.6	121.0	(136.0)	(144.5)	144.5	(174.0)	(197.0)	198.5

Note: Details may not add to totals due to rounding.
[a] Figures listed under "proposed 1966" are from the President's budget message; those listed as projections for 1968 and 1973 are based on our own assumptions for the models as given in the text.
[b] Figures in parentheses are estimates that appear unrealistic in the absence of additional measures. See also Table 2, p. 9.

prepared for this period for the administrative budget and for the receipts side of the federal government sector in the national income accounts. With some minor exceptions described under the individual tax sources, no changes in tax legislation beyond those foreshadowed in the President's 1966 budget have been incorporated in the estimates. Even though it is not reflected in the estimates, however, it is assumed that a further tax reduction, or alternatively a tax sharing, will take place during the period of the projections.

The Individual Income Tax

Models II-A and II-B assume a small decline in the proportion of GNP represented by personal income, from about 79.6 percent of GNP in 1963 to about 78.0 percent in 1973. Conversely, small increases have been assumed in the shares represented by corporate profits, depreciation, and indirect business taxes. These shifts do not apply to Model I, where such relationships are projected to remain practically unchanged.

All models show a rise in actual tax collections for every year. However, because of the recent (1964) tax cut, the percentage of total GNP claimed by the individual income tax remains below the 1963 level throughout the entire period covered by the study. In 1973 this tax will claim about 7.5 percent of GNP in all models, whereas the 1963 figure was 8.4 percent. In dollar terms, collections would rise from $47.6 billion in 1963 to a 1973 level of $69.0 billion in Model I and $76.2 billion in Models II-A and II-B. The individual income tax would account for well over 50 percent of total federal administrative budget receipts in all models.

Corporate Profits Tax

Ever since its enactment in 1909, the corporate profits tax has been the most volatile of tax sources, fluctuating greatly with the ups and downs of the business cycle, generally with a lag of about six to nine months (reflecting the lag of tax collections behind accruals).

Our models take account of the reductions in corporate profits tax rates of the years 1963-64 and the gradual advance of payment dates to put the tax for larger corporations on an almost current basis. Consequently it seemed desirable to align corporate tax receipts with current fiscal year GNP and corporate profits figures in each case, whereas hitherto it has been the practice to compare such receipts with GNP and profit figures of the preceding calendar year.

In Models II-A and II-B our calculations assume an immediately rising profits trend in relation to GNP, to slightly under 10 percent of GNP, where it is assumed to remain broadly unchanged through 1973. (All figures are for fiscal years.) For Model I the profits trend is assumed to be considerably less favorable because the economy would be generally less prosperous, and projected profits would amount to only 8.0 percent of GNP in 1973.

In absolute terms, by 1973 the yield of the corporate profits tax is projected to reach a level of $40.9 billion (over 4 percent of GNP) for Models II-A and II-B, and $32 billion for Model I. This would constitute approximately 28 percent of total federal administrative budget revenues for the "full employment" models, but only about 25.5 percent in the case of Model I.

Excise Taxes

We have assumed that the proposals in the President's budget message for a reduction in excise taxes as of July 1, 1965, will be enacted, but that no further changes in existing legislation will take place. The only exception concerns gasoline and other highway excises, which Models I and II-A assume will continue at present rates throughout the period under study. (At present the gasoline tax is scheduled to drop to 1.5 cents a gallon on October 1, 1972.) Model II-B assumes a tax rise of 1 cent a gallon starting in fiscal 1970 to pay for an extended highway program. In absolute terms, the rise in excise taxes (in Table 10, "excise taxes" plus "gasoline and other highway excises") from fiscal 1966 to fiscal 1973 is from $13.8 billion to $19.4 billion in Model I, $21.4 billion in Model II-A, and $22.5 billion in Model II-B.

The old traditional taxes on alcohol, tobacco, and documents (the last one is unimportant) are projected to show less-than-average increases, although in all cases they show substantial growth in absolute terms.

Excise taxes will continue to be an important component of total federal revenues, accounting for over 10 percent of total receipts from the public in 1973 in all the models.

Estate and Gift Taxes

Estate and gift taxes have been assumed to rise more than in proportion to the rise in GNP because of the fact that a rising percentage of deceased persons will leave taxable estates and also because of the element of progressiveness in the application of these taxes. The yield depends in large part on asset values—stocks, real estate, etc. For these reasons, receipts in Model I are projected at considerably lower levels than in Models II-A and II-B because such asset values are likely to be lower in an economy with a slower rate of growth. Their yield is projected to increase from $3.2 billion to $3.9 billion between fiscal 1966 and fiscal 1973 in Model I and to $6 billion in Models II-A and II-B. In terms of percentages of GNP, the increase is significant only in the last two models. And even in these models, the share of estate and gift tax receipts in total federal administrative budget revenues would amount to only about 4 percent. It must be remembered that increases in this category are held down because credits on federal taxes are granted for state gift and inheritance taxes, and it has been assumed that by 1973 virtually all the states will have increased these taxes to the point where the maximum possible federal credit is applicable.

Customs Duties

The revenue yield of customs duties depends on two factors: general economic conditions and United States tariff policy. It has been assumed here that reasonably full employment conditions will mean a more-than-proportionate increase in the dollar value of imports and that this will be only slightly offset by a further lowering of tariffs. A recent Brookings study[1] indicates that prices of imports will probably rise more than prices of exports.

Customs receipts are expected to rise from $1.5 billion in fiscal 1966 to $2.6 billion in 1973 (only $2.2 billion for Model I), but even by that date, they will represent less than 0.3 percent of total GNP and less than 2 percent of administrative budget revenues.

[1] Walter S. Salant and Emile Despres, Lawrence B. Krause, Alice M. Rivlin, William A. Salant, Lorie Tarshis, *The United States Balance of Payments in 1968* (Brookings Institution, 1963).

Miscellaneous Receipts

Miscellaneous sources, including such items as interest on loans, dividends and deposit earnings, and sales of products and property, are so mixed and there are so many uncertain items—particularly those arising from the disposition of federally owned assets (including the strategic stockpile which was accumulated largely on the basis of World War II requirements)—that detailed forecasts become meaningless. It has therefore been assumed that such receipts will show only small increases during the period.

Trust Fund Receipts

Model I projections of employment taxes and voluntary payments by the states for their employees have been worked out on the basis of the existing law, incorporating all scheduled increases. Also included are the increases in social security tax rates and in its tax base proposed by the President, as well as the proposed taxes to finance Medicare for the Aged and to improve the unemployment insurance system. No further increases in rates or base have been assumed. For all the calculations a 3 percent annual increase in wage rates has been assumed, while for current dollar models an additional annual price increase of 1.5 percent is included (1.3 percent for Model I). With unchanged ceilings for contributions, this means that a slowly declining percentage of all wage and salary payments will be covered.

Model I estimates are based on a study by Robert J. Myers.[2] It was assumed that the increase in receipts due to the 1.3 percent annual price increase projected in the model would just about offset the decrease in revenues due to the assumed higher rate of unemployment, since Myers' figures are based on reasonably full employment with no change in prices. For Models II-A and II-B slight increases were projected because of the assumption of an increased

[2] Robert J. Myers, "Actuarial Cost Estimates for the Hospital Insurance Act of 1965 and Social Security Amendments of 1965," Actuarial Study No. 59 (U.S. Department of Health, Education, and Welfare, 1965). See also the *25th Annual Report of Federal Old-Age and Survivors Insurance and Disability Insurance Trust Funds* (Social Security Trust Fund, Board of Trustees, 1965).

labor force and lower unemployment, as well as slightly greater price increases. The arms reduction model shows a further small increase because of its slightly higher civilian labor force.

Employment taxes are projected to constitute a rising portion of federal cash receipts, increasing from $18.7 billion, or 2.8 percent of GNP, in fiscal 1966 to $33.8 billion (Model I) and $36.9 billion (Model II-B) by 1973, at which time they would account for about 3.6 percent of GNP. By far the greatest portion of such receipts will consist of contributions to the OASI and Disability Insurance trust funds. Contributions to the Railroad Retirement fund will decline slightly though by no means in line with the recent and anticipated future decline in railroad employment, as it was felt that this development would not have its full impact on these funds until well after 1973.

Employment taxes will constitute a steadily rising percentage of all federal receipts, rising from 13.6 percent in fiscal 1963 to between 18.5 and 19.3 percent ten years later. However, it should be pointed out that under less favorable employment conditions, employment tax revenues would fall considerably short of the levels projected here. But, of course, the same observation applies to all other tax sources.

For Models II-A and II-B, which are based on the assumption of reasonably full employment, the figures show only a slight rise in unemployment tax deposits by states during the later years of the decade, because of increases in the labor force. It was felt that even increasing the earnings base for calculating contributions would not make any significant difference, as under existing legislation most states would be likely to reduce their tax rates on covered earnings correspondingly. With nearly full employment, the estimates here are compatible with continuous small increases in the benefits provided by the individual states. Model I figures are somewhat higher throughout, because the slower rate of growth inherent in that model would cause a higher rate of unemployment and this would require larger tax deposits by the states in spite of an increasing share of federal support for this purpose.

Employee and agency contributions to the civil service retirement fund (in Table 10, these are included in the "other" category) are bound to rise slowly year by year, and they have been projected accordingly.

CHAPTER VI

Projections of
Federal Expenditures

IN THIS AND THE remaining chapters we undertake to project the expenditures side of the federal budget. In this chapter the general assumptions underlying the projections are detailed. In Chapters VII through X the estimates under the various models are given by functional classifications grouped under the broad categories of national security, economic development, welfare, and general government operations.

Our expenditure estimates follow the general assumptions outlined in Chapter I. Except in Model I they postulate the approximation of reasonably full employment (no more than 4 percent of the labor force unemployed) toward the end of fiscal 1967 and the economy's ability to sustain this level of employment thereafter.

On the domestic scene, it is assumed that there will be no change in the division of functions performed by the federal government and by state and local governments. In regard to world affairs, one set of estimates is based on a continuation of the present defense posture, while a second set assumes that there will be some reduction in defense expenditures.

Definitions of the three models presented were given in Chapter I, and the various combinations of defense and nondefense expenditure levels were also described. Expenditure details have been worked out under several different classifications.

The first classification shows expenditures by function and is further subdivided by government agency under each functional category. These estimates have been developed in detail, but are presented here in summary form.

Because of space limitations, the classification of expenditures by agency is presented in the appendix tables, and this too is in summary form. For the same reason, the object classification, although prepared in detail, is not presented.

Expenditure Estimates by Budget Concept and Functional Category

Tables 11 and 12 present our expenditure models on the consolidated cash and the national income accounts bases for selected years. Year-by-year tables for these, as well as for administrative budget expenditures, are in the appendix (Tables A-15, A-16, and A-17 for expenditures). The consolidated cash budget table (Table 11) is subdivided into broad functional classifications which have been grouped into the four "super-categories" of national security (including space and international), economic development (including education), welfare (including agriculture), and general government operations (including interest). The chapters that follow are also based on these four classifications.

As is apparent from Table 11, our projections show very substantial shifts among the various classes of expenditures during the period under study. To a certain extent, such a shift is already taking place. National security expenditures are expected to decline from 46.9 percent of cash budget expenditures in fiscal 1963 to 41.2 percent in fiscal 1966 if proposed programs are carried out. By contrast, the tables show substantial increases in economic development and welfare expenditures. In our projections these trends become more pronounced. Security expenditures make up 32.5 to 37.2 percent of all projected budgetary expenditures in fiscal 1968 and between 22.0 and 31.9 percent of all such expenditures in fiscal 1973. Significant increases in relative importance are shown by expenditures for economic development (particularly for education), which gain from 8.2 percent in fiscal 1966 to between 13.2 and

15.1 percent of all cash budget expenditures in fiscal 1973, and by welfare expenditures, which are projected to rise from 32.0 percent to between 41.0 and 46.6 percent of all outlays during the same period.

Expressed in terms of the national income accounts (see Table 12) our projections show the greatest increases in transfer payments (mainly all kinds of social insurance and interest) and in grants-in-aid to state and local governments. These payments increase substantially because of much greater outlays in the categories of commerce and transportation (the interstate highways program is financed by means of grants-in-aid), housing and community development, health research and services, economic opportunity programs, public welfare services, and education and research. In all these categories no change is envisaged in present federal-state-local relationships; and in Models II-A and II-B, for most new programs, it is assumed that the direct federal role will be kept to a minimum in favor of state and local responsibility.

Model I

Why do the projections show an increase in expenditures even in the model which excludes adoption of new programs? For one thing, we assume gradually rising prices; and, more important, many existing programs imply increasing expenditures. This is the case, for example, with certain grant-in-aid programs that match rising state expenditures. It is true even more of many new programs proposed by President Johnson that are now included in the budget with relatively small initial amounts and for which expenditures will rise in future years. Table 13, showing planned expenditures for fiscal 1966 for some of these new programs and the new obligational authority requested for them, offers a good illustration of what may be expected in future years.

Finally, the impact of some factors that have tended to reduce recorded expenditures in recent years will necessarily diminish. This applies particularly to the sale of assets by such agencies as the Veterans Administration, the Federal Housing Administration, the Department of Agriculture, and the Export-Import Bank.

On the other hand, some reduction in expenditures may result from the phasing out of existing programs (for example, the program for hardening missile sites) or from increased efficiency. While

TABLE 11. Model I and Model II: Federal Expenditures in Cash Budget by Four Major Categories, 1963, 1966, 1968, and 1973

(In billions of current dollars for fiscal years)

Item	Actual 1963	Proposed 1966	Projected 1968					Projected 1973			
			Model I	Model II-A1	Model II-A2	Model II-B	Model I	Model II-A1	Model II-A2	Model II-B
National security, international, and space										
National security activities[a]	53.4	52.5	52.8	52.8	49.7	49.7	53.3	53.3	43.5	43.5
International affairs and finance	3.8	4.2	4.8	5.5	5.5	7.0	5.5	8.5	8.5	11.8
Space research and technology	2.6	5.1	6.0	4.0	4.0	7.0	6.0	4.0	4.0	6.5
Total	59.8	61.8	63.6	62.3	59.2	63.7	64.8	65.8	56.0	61.8
As a percentage of total expenditures	51.7	47.9	44.0	41.9	40.7	41.0	38.0	35.6	31.8	30.8
Economic development										
Natural resources	2.5	2.9	3.3	3.6	3.6	3.9	3.9	4.4	4.4	5.0
Commerce and transportation	5.8	6.5	8.1	8.7	8.7	9.2	10.4	11.5	11.5	12.9
Education and research	1.2	2.6	4.3	4.8	4.8	5.3	8.0	9.5	9.5	12.5
Total	9.5	12.0	15.7	17.1	17.1	18.4	22.3	25.4	25.4	30.4
As a percentage of total expenditures	8.2	9.3	11.1	11.7	12.0	12.0	13.2	13.8	14.6	15.1

78

Welfare									
Agriculture	5.7	5.0	4.6	4.6	4.3	5.0	4.6	4.6	4.1
Housing and community development	-0.3	1.6	2.3	2.3	3.0	2.8	4.0	4.0	6.9
Health research and services	1.3	2.8	3.2	3.2	3.7	4.7	5.5	5.5	7.2
Labor and manpower[b]	3.5	4.2	4.4	4.4	5.1	7.4	6.2	6.2	7.8
Economic opportunity programs	—	1.9	2.4	2.4	2.8	3.7	4.3	4.3	5.5
Public welfare services	3.1	4.6	5.3	5.3	6.4	5.7	6.9	6.9	9.0
Social insurance[c]	17.8	26.0	27.5	27.5	28.0	33.3	39.5	39.5	45.5
Veterans' benefits and services	6.0	6.1	6.7	6.7	6.7	7.0	7.8	7.8	7.8
Total	37.1	52.2	56.4	56.4	60.0	69.6	78.8	78.8	93.8
As a percentage of total expenditures	32.0	36.3	38.2	38.7	38.7	41.0	42.5	45.0	46.6
General government operations									
General government	2.0	2.7	3.1	3.1	3.1	3.5	4.3	4.3	4.3
Interest on the federal debt	7.4	9.6	9.6	9.5	9.8	10.0	10.5	10.5	10.7
Total	9.4	12.3	12.7	12.6	12.9	13.5	14.8	14.8	15.0
As a percentage of total expenditures	8.1	8.6	8.2	8.6	8.3	7.8	8.1	8.6	7.5
Total, cash budget expenditures	115.8	143.8	148.5	145.3	155.0	170.2	184.8	175.0	201.0
Less: adjustments[d]	-2.0	-2.0	-2.0	-2.0	-2.0	-2.5	-2.5	-2.5	-2.5
Total, adjusted cash budget expenditures	113.8	141.8	146.5	143.3	153.0	167.7	182.3	172.5	198.5

a Includes military functions of the Department of Defense, military assistance, the Atomic Energy Commission, and other defense-related activities.
b Includes unemployment compensation.
c Excludes unemployment compensation.
d These include a number of items which cannot be assigned to any specific category. The largest items are negative amounts—connected with the accounting treatment of agency expenditures and salary deductions for retirement of federal employees.

TABLE 12. Model I and Model II: Federal Expenditures in the National Income Accounts, 1963, 1966, 1968, and 1973

(In billions of current dollars for fiscal years)

Item	Actual 1963	Proposed 1966	Projected 1968				Projected 1973			
			Model I	Model II-A1	Model II-A2	Model II-B	Model I	Model II-A1	Model II-A2	Model II-B
Purchases of goods and services	63.6	66.7	70.5	72.5	69.5	73.2	77.5	79.0	70.5	76.0
Transfer payments	29.2	35.2	41.5	43.0	43.0	45.2	52.5	62.0	62.0	73.8
Grants-in-aid to state and local governments	8.3	13.0	17.5	18.5	18.5	20.5	23.5	26.0	26.0	33.5
Net interest paid	7.4	8.6	9.5	9.5	9.5	9.6	10.0	10.5	10.5	10.7
Subsidies less current surplus of government enterprises	3.8	3.5	3.5	3.5	3.5	3.5	3.5	3.5	3.5	3.0
Total	112.3	127.0	142.5	147.0	144.0	152.0	167.0	181.0	172.5	197.0
Total expenditures as a percentage of GNP	19.8	18.6	19.3	19.1	18.7	19.7	18.1	18.0	17.1	19.6

TABLE 13. Major Additions to Federal Programs Proposed in the President's Budget for Fiscal Year 1966[a]

(In millions of current dollars)

Item	Administration's proposed expenditures	New obligational authority requested
International		
Investment in Inter-American Development Bank	25	250
Commerce and transportation		
Surface transport research	10	20
Area Redevelopment Administration	40	400
Post Office: direct federal construction	18	92
Education		
Assistance to elementary and secondary education	500	1,255
Academic facilities loans and grants[b]	165	642
Assistance to colleges and college students	100	260
Agriculture		
Rural housing insurance fund	40	100
Housing and community development		
Public assistance grants	15	150
Urban mass transportation[c]	48	161
Health		
Health centers, etc.	95	191
Labor		
Broadened and extended Manpower Development and Training Act	92	140
Economic Opportunity programs[d]	1,346	1,500
Public welfare services		
Public assistance: increased federal share, expanded medical assistance to needy children, etc.	214	214
Other: expanded vocational rehabilitation	7	10
Total	2,715	5,385

[a] Proposals relating to social insurance are not included.
[b] Enacted in 1964, but it is estimated that only $3 million will be spent in fiscal 1965.
[c] This item is not new, but there have been no major expenditures previously.
[d] Some initial funds for the attack on poverty were included in the 1965 budget.

we cannot be certain that our estimates strike the right balance between the built-in increases and probable economies, it is clear that the former will average between $5 and $6 billion annually in the cash budget, based on existing and officially proposed legislation only.

TABLE 14. Model II: Federal Expenditures, Showing Increases over Model I for New or Changed Programs[a], Cash Budget, 1968 and 1973

(In billions of current dollars for fiscal years)

Item	Projected 1968		Projected 1973	
	Model II-A	Model II-B	Model II-A	Model II-B
National security: gradual arms reduction[b]	-3.1	-3.1	-9.8	-9.8
International affairs and finance				
International police force	0.2	0.8	1.0	2.4
Increased economic assistance	0.1	0.7	1.4	2.9
Space research and technology				
Reduced lunar program (stretch-out)	-2.0		-2.0	
Accelerated lunar and increased interplanetary programs		1.0		0.5
Natural resources: larger recreation programs	0.1	0.1	0.1	0.3
Commerce and transportation				
Increased highway construction				1.0
Increased regional development programs (more areas)	0.2	0.4	0.3	0.6
Post Office deficit decrease				-0.5
Education and research: increased assistance to—				
Elementary and secondary education	0.2	0.4	0.5	1.2
Higher education	0.2	0.5	0.5	2.0
Vocational education		0.1	0.1	0.2
National Science Foundation	0.1	0.1	0.1	0.3
New research programs not elsewhere classified	0.1	0.2	0.2	0.6
Agriculture: smaller support programs	-0.4	-0.7	-0.4	-0.9

Program				
Housing and community development				
Increased urban mass transportation programs	0.1	0.1	0.1	0.5
Increased urban renewal	0.1	0.3	0.3	0.8
Increased public housing, "spot" renewal, rent subsidy plan	0.1	0.2	0.3	0.7
Contingency fund		0.1		0.3
Health				
New research programs for National Institutes of Health	0.1	0.2	0.1	0.5
Expanded Public Health Service and other new health programs	0.3	0.5	0.7	1.6
Labor				
Expanded manpower programs	0.1	0.3	0.3	0.8
Expanded and liberalized unemployment benefits	0.1	0.6	0.5	1.2
Economic opportunity				
Larger Community Action programs	0.1	0.2	0.2	0.6
Expanded Job Corps	0.1	0.2	0.2	0.5
Expanded work-training programs and others	0.2	0.4	0.3	0.8
Public welfare services				
New "general" welfare grants	0.4	1.1	0.6	1.9
Expanded "nationwide" Food Stamp program	0.1	0.1	0.5	0.5
Increased vocational rehabilitation and others	0.1	0.4	0.1	0.6
Contingency fund		0.1		0.3
Social insurance				
Increased social security benefits	0.4	0.8	2.2	4.3
Increased Medicare for the Aged	0.1	0.2	0.2	0.4
Increased civil service and railroad retirement pensions	0.1	0.2	0.2	0.4
General Medicare; private health insurance premium subsidy				2.5
Veterans benefits and services: liberalized benefits	0.6	0.6	0.8	0.8
General government: various programs such as public defenders and compensation for crimes of violence	0.1	0.1	0.2	0.2

a For comparison, see Model I projected expenditures in Table 11.
b Not applicable to Model II-A1.

83

Model II

Model II-A incorporates a number of new programs, in addition to those included in Model I. This results in higher expenditures, although it is assumed that a few programs, notably in agriculture, will decline somewhat. There are two variations to this model. The first (Model II-A1) shows the same amount of defense expenditures as Model I, while in the second (Model II-A2) defense expenditures are cut back by nearly $10 billion from 1966 to 1973.

Model II-B may be called the "civilian high-expenditure model." It contains all the new programs also included in Model II-A, but projects that they will be initiated faster and on a larger scale. In addition, in a few instances it contains expenditures for programs that are not included in the Model II-A estimates because it has been assumed for the latter model that they will not begin until after fiscal 1973. As may be seen from Table 14, the principal program increases for all models are concentrated heavily in the welfare and economic development fields. Under these programs considerable assistance would be given to state and local governments, thus enabling them to carry out their steadily growing functions with a much lower tax load than would be possible without federal support.

Federal Government Civilian Personnel

Our projections assume a negligible rise in federal employment during the period 1964-73. Reductions in civilian employment for the Department of Defense just about offset smaller increases in most other agencies dealing with civilian tasks. Fluctuations are introduced by the temporary requirements of the Census Bureau, but the over-all figure for federal civilian employment is expected to stay close to the 2.5 million mark.[1] Additional factors responsible for this relative stability of employment in the face of rising dollar expenditures are the anticipated increases in the productivity of federal employees, and the greater emphasis on transfer payments and on grants-in-aid to the states. This applies particularly to Model II-B. For these categories of expenditures, little additional manpower

[1] For details, see Appendix Table A-4.

would be needed at the federal level, since the actual administration of most programs would be at the state or local level. Thus there might be some further increase in nondefense employment in all variations of Model II, but in Models II-A2 and II-B it would be offset by lower civilian employment in the Department of Defense.

CHAPTER VII

Military, International, and Space Programs

THIS CHAPTER DEALS with expenditures for the military functions of the Department of Defense, for the Atomic Energy Commission, and the National Aeronautics and Space Administration. Also included are the expenditures of the various departments and agencies active in the international field. Prominent among these are the Department of State, the Agency for International Development, the U.S. Information Agency, the U.S. Arms Control and Disarmament Agency, and several minor commissions. The Peace Corps and the Export-Import Bank, the Food-for-Peace program, and support for international financial institutions also fall in this category.

National Security Expenditures

Department of Defense

The international political climate will be the principal factor determining the size of the Department of Defense over the next decade. In recent years increases in the budget have been triggered by heightened tension over Berlin, Cuba, and Viet Nam, to name but three examples. Longer-run trends will be influenced decisively by a variety of factors, such as the military posture of the Soviet Union or Communist China, developments in defense technology, and the state of public opinion concerning them. (See Table 15.)

In Models I and II-A1, we have assumed that present world tensions will continue, with neither a deterioration nor a significant improvement in international relations. Hence we have projected a constant figure of about $50 billion for the Department of Defense budget over the decade. While this figure was chosen to imply a continuation of present policies, it actually represents a somewhat smaller defense budget in real terms, particularly for the later years of the decade, if annual price increases are taken into account.

On the other hand, we assume in Models II-A2 and II-B that there will be a moderate, gradual reduction in arms expenditures to a level of around $40 billion in current dollars by 1973. This corresponds to a somewhat stretched-out version of the degree of arms reduction suggested by Deputy Secretary of Defense Gilpatric.[1]

Because of their large size and their importance for the American economy, Department of Defense expenditures have been broken down and projected in a number of different ways: by Program, a concept introduced recently by Secretary McNamara and Assistant Secretary Hitch (see Table 16) and by Appropriation Account, which was the traditional way of presenting the accounts of the Department of Defense (see Table 17). Projections of both methods of presentation are useful for an understanding of future defense needs.

For the period under review, United States defense requirements may be grouped under the following broad categories: (1) a strategic defense force that could ward off or absorb a nuclear attack and retaliate by destroying the enemy with controlled precision, (2) conventional forces (ground, naval, and air) sufficient to meet threats ranging from guerrilla warfare to continental-sized conflicts; and (3) a research and development program to develop new weapons systems to perform existing tasks better and meet new challenges.

[1] Roswell L. Gilpatric, "Our Defense Needs: The Long View," *Foreign Affairs* (April 1964).

TABLE 15. Federal Expenditures for National Security Activities, Administrative Budget[a], 1963-73

(In billions of current and constant fiscal 1963 dollars)

| Fiscal year | Present policy, actual and projected[b] | | | | | Arms reduction alternative[b] | | | | |
| | Current dollars | | | As a percentage of GNP[f] | Constant dollars[c] Total | Current dollars | | | As a percentage of GNP | Constant dollars[c] Total |
	Total[d]	Defense Dept.[e]	Atomic Energy Comm.			Total[d]	Defense Dept.[e]	Atomic Energy Comm.		
1963	52.8	50.0	2.8	9.3	52.8					
1964	54.2	51.2	2.8	9.0	53.3					
1965	52.2	49.3	2.7	8.2	50.6					
1966	51.6	49.0	2.5	7.6	49.3					
1967	51.7	49.0	2.6	7.1	48.7	50.7	48.0	2.6	7.0	47.7
1968	51.8	49.0	2.7	6.7	48.1	49.2	46.5	2.6	6.4	45.6
1969	51.9	49.0	2.8	6.4	47.4	48.3	45.5	2.7	5.9	44.1
1970	52.0	49.0	2.9	6.1	46.8	46.9	44.0	2.8	5.5	42.2
1971	52.1	49.0	3.0	5.8	46.2	45.4	42.5	2.8	5.0	40.3
1972	52.2	49.0	3.1	5.5	45.6	44.0	41.0	2.9	4.6	38.5
1973	52.3	49.0	3.2	5.2	45.0	43.0	40.0	3.0	4.3	37.0

[a] Trust fund expenditures for national security (principally arms bought by foreign nations for cash) have been projected at $1 billion annually for the "present policy" and at $0.5 billion annually for the "arms reduction alternative." These amounts should be added to the figures in this table to obtain consolidated cash budget figures.

[b] The assumptions used for projections under "present policy" are roughly comparable to those of Model I and Model II-A1; those under "arms reduction" are closer to Model II-A2 and Model II-B.

[c] Calculated by using the price deflators assumed for Model II.

[d] Includes a small amount for defense-related activities of agencies other than the Defense Department and the Atomic Energy Commission.

[e] Includes Department of Defense military functions and military assistance.

[f] The projected GNP for Model II was used to calculate this percentage.

TABLE 16. Expenditures of Department of Defense by Program[a], Total Obligational Availability, 1963, 1966, 1968, and 1973

(In billions of current dollars for fiscal years)

Item	Actual 1963	Proposed 1966	Projected 1968		Projected 1973	
			Present policy[b]	Arms reduction[c]	Present policy[b]	Arms reduction[c]
Strategic retaliatory forces	8.4	4.5	4.0	3.0	4.0	1.2
Continental air and missile defense forces	1.9	1.8	1.7	1.6	1.5	1.5
General purpose forces	17.9	19.0	19.0	17.7	18.2	15.0
Sealift and airlift forces	1.4	1.6	1.5	1.3	1.5	1.0
Reserve and guard forces	1.8	2.0	2.0	2.0	2.0	1.0
Research and development	5.1	5.4	5.5	5.4	5.5	5.0
General support	13.1	14.6	14.2	13.4	13.6	12.3
Retired pay	1.0	1.5	1.8	2.0	2.5	3.0
Civil defense	0.1	0.1	0.1	0.1	0.1	0.1
Military assistance	1.6	1.1	1.2	1.0	1.1	0.9
Total obligational availability	52.2	51.6	51.0	47.5	50.0	41.0
Adjustment to expenditures	−2.2	−2.6	−2.0	−1.0	−1.0	−1.0
Total expenditures	50.0	49.0	49.0	46.5	49.0	40.0

Note: Details may not add to totals due to rounding.
[a] Expenditures for military assistance have been included.
[b] The assumptions used for "present policy" are roughly comparable to those of Model I and Model II-A1.
[c] The assumptions for "arms reduction" are closest to those of Model II-A2 and Model II-B.

STRATEGIC RETALIATORY FORCES. Long-range bombers, their guided missiles, tankers, and decoys; intercontinental ballistic missiles; and ballistic missile submarines with their auxiliary ships make up the strategic retaliatory forces. The main thrust of the strategic program must be to replace obsolescent planes (such as the B-47) and "soft" missiles with hardened missiles (Minuteman) and submarine-launched missiles (Polaris and Poseidon). By 1968 this program should be virtually completed, and it is increasingly difficult to forecast the trend of expenditures for this category after that year. Everything will depend on future decisions. Two developments that might entail considerable expenditures are the introduction of an advanced ICBM capable of penetrating missile defenses and the production of a new strategic deep-sea submarine.

Expenditures for strategic retaliatory forces reached a peak of

$9.1 billion in 1962. Since then, they have been declining steadily, and further reductions have been assumed for both of our models. This is particularly pronounced for Models II-A2 and II-B (arms reduction models) because of our assumption that the most severe cuts will take place in this category of weapons. In these models most expenditures for this program are assumed to be of a maintenance nature only.

TABLE 17. Expenditures of Department of Defense by Appropriation Account[a], Administrative Budget, 1963, 1966, 1968, and 1973

(In billions of current dollars for fiscal years)

Item	Actual 1963	Proposed 1966	Projected 1968		Projected 1973	
			Present policy[b]	Arms reduction[c]	Present policy[b]	Arms reduction[c]
Military personnel	13.0	14.8	15.5	15.1	17.0	14.0
Operations and maintenance	11.9	12.2	13.0	12.5	13.0	10.7
Procurement	16.6	13.2	12.0	11.0	11.0	8.0
Research, development, testing, and evaluation	6.4	6.4	6.5	6.5	6.5	6.0
Military construction	1.1	0.9	0.8	0.5	0.7	0.3
Family housing	0.4	0.7	0.4	0.2	0.3	0.2
Civil defense	0.2	0.1	0.1	0.1	0.1	0.1
Military assistance	1.7	1.1	1.2	1.1	1.1	0.8
Revolving and management funds	−1.4	−0.4	−0.5	−0.5	−0.7	−0.1
Total	50.0	49.0	49.0	46.5	49.0	40.0

Note: Details may not add to totals due to rounding.
[a] Expenditures for military assistance have been included.
[b] The assumptions used for "present policy" are roughly comparable to those of Model I and Model II-A1.
[c] The assumptions for "arms reduction" are closest to those of Model II-A2 and Model II-B.

CONTINENTAL AIR AND MISSILE DEFENSE FORCES. The continental air and missile defense program is composed of the weapons systems, warning and communications networks, and auxiliary equipment that are required to detect, identify, track, and destroy hostile forces approaching the North American continent. The defense forces will always constitute an important part of any security system, and they will be constantly upgraded. However, the rate of modernization is subject to discretion, as is the introduction of completely new weapons systems. Thus the F-111 interceptor plane will find its place here, and at some time during the period a decision will have to be made whether or not to introduce a general anti-missile defense system (Nike X) to strengthen the defenses in this category.

Differences between the models in expenditure projections for this program are fairly small, since even in case of some relaxation of tension most of these defense forces are likely to be retained. Slight reductions are projected in all models for this category.

GENERAL PURPOSE FORCES. General purpose forces include most Army and Navy combat and combat support units, all Marine Corps units, and the tactical units of the Air Force. Their mission is to carry out the entire range of military operations short of general nuclear war, from guerrilla-type actions and naval blockades to large-scale, though limited, wars anywhere in the world. The experience of the recent past does not suggest that conventional forces are likely to be eclipsed. On the contrary, events in Southeast Asia, the Congo, the Near East, and other trouble spots show the need for conventional forces, and both our models take account of this.

Therefore, only relatively small reductions in Army personnel have been assumed, but greater cutbacks have been assumed for Navy and especially for Air Force personnel. The strength of the Marine Corps has been projected as constant because the Corps serves to give maximum flexibility in any situation.

It is easier to project total expenditures for general purpose forces than to try to distribute the total among the various components. Obviously under any arms reduction program, general purpose forces will be less affected than will most other categories, and this is brought out in our models. However, it is not possible at this stage to predict whether the Army will have more airlift or tactical fighter programs under its own umbrella or whether these will continue to appear under Air Force appropriations. Similarly it is difficult to forecast the rate of replacement of naval vessels, although it appears that under both of our assumptions the absolute strength of the fleet is bound to decline. During the period until 1973 the United States will have to decide whether or not to embark on a major program for replacing existing vessels with nuclear powered ships. The size of the naval construction budget will depend to a great extent on the timing of such a decision. However, a continuation of the present level of expenditures for the ship replacement program is assumed in Model I, and there is only a very moderate reduction in replacement expenditures in Models II-A2 and II-B.

SEALIFT AND AIRLIFT FORCES. Sealift and airlift forces complement the general purpose forces, providing prompt transportation wherever it is needed. The program should continue to enjoy a high priority for funds because of the great importance of maximum mobility.

RESERVE AND GUARD FORCES. The strength of reserve and guard forces is projected as somewhat less than its June 1964 level of 1,048,000 members.

RESEARCH AND DEVELOPMENT. In projecting the budget for research and development, there are no data on cost and workload or future plans by which an analyst can estimate future expenditures. Attempts might be made to minimize duplication between Department of Defense and National Aeronautics and Space Administration expenditures. This study assumes that research programs will continue at a fairly high level, mainly to keep facilities and know-how permanently available to serve whatever future needs might arise. Models II-A2 and II-B assume some cutback in development expenditures during later years.

GENERAL SUPPORT. The general support program is the residual category that contains all supporting activities of the military services not allocated directly to the other major programs. It includes individual training and education, communications, logistic support, medical services, command and control, support of nuclear weapons programs, and miscellaneous activities. All these functions will remain important, and changes in expenditures on them will depend on changes in the entire defense program. Hence a reduction in expenditures is shown in the arms reduction alternative.

RETIRED PAY. The numbers of retired military personnel are projected to grow by about 50 percent between 1963 and 1968, and they will continue to grow, though at a somewhat slower rate, through 1973. Rates of retired pay have been assumed to increase at the same rate as regular military pay and civil service salaries generally.

CIVIL DEFENSE. An effective civil defense program could increase greatly the number of persons surviving a nuclear attack, particularly in combination with an effective anti-missile missile. So far Congress has treated civil defense expenditures as a stepchild, and while there is no reason at the present time to expect any change, a change in attitude could compel larger expenditures in this field in the future.

MILITARY ASSISTANCE. More than sixty countries receive grants and loans under the military assistance program, although in 1966 nearly three-quarters of the total amount will go to 11 of these countries. Its continuation throughout the decade has been assumed, although on a somewhat reduced scale because of tighter controls and other developments. The more affluent noncommunist countries will continue to pay cash for the weapons they purchase in the United States. Such purchases account for by far the biggest item of trust fund expenditures in the field of national security.

BREAKDOWN OF EXPENDITURES BY APPROPRIATION ACCOUNT. The appropriation accounts are the traditional form in which the Defense Department's budget is presented to, and acted upon by, the Congress. Projections for the various categories by appropriation account are shown in Table 17.

Expenditure estimates for military personnel follow the manpower estimates in Table 18. It has been assumed that military pay will rise in line with civil service pay generally. Expenditures for operations and maintenance have been assumed to remain on a fairly steady base, but rather large reductions in procurement expenditures have been projected. These cuts are particularly large in Models II-A2 and II-B, because arms reduction plans are bound to cut heavily into procurement. By contrast, research, development, test, and evaluation expenditures have been left relatively undisturbed, whereas family housing and military construction, it is assumed, will be cut back considerably.

TABLE 18. Defense Manpower Requirements, 1964, 1968, and 1973

(In thousands, fiscal years)

Branch	Actual 1964[a]	Projected 1968		Projected 1973	
		Present policy[b]	Arms reduction[c]	Present policy[b]	Arms reduction[c]
Army	972	940	900	900	800
Navy	667	620	570	570	460
Marine Corps	190	190	190	190	190
Air Force	856	750	690	600	420
Total active	2,685	2,500	2,350	2,260	1,870
Civilian[d]	998	900	850	800	700
Reserve and National Guard	1,048	1,000	1,000	950	900
Retired	411	625	650	875	1,050

[a] As of June.
[b] The assumptions for "present policy" are roughly comparable to those of Model I and Model II-A1.
[c] The assumptions for "arms reduction" are closest to those of Model II-A2 and Model II-B.
[d] Civilian employment for military functions and military assistance.

Atomic Energy Commission

The Atomic Energy Commission undertakes two distinct kinds of activities. The first group is primarily defense-related, such as the procurement and production of nuclear materials and of atomic weapons as well as the development of military and space reactors. The second group comprises the development of civilian power reactors, most of its varied research, and all of its other activities devoted to peaceful uses of atomic energy. (See Table 19.)

Both our models reflect a stretch-out in procurement of nuclear materials that is primarily defense-related and a scheduled drop in the price of uranium. Furthermore, it is assumed that during the later years of the decade the AEC will acquire raw materials only for its own use. A larger cutback in weapons development is assumed in Models II-A2 and II-B, for which higher civilian expenditures are projected.

Specifically, it is assumed that major advances will be made in the civilian reactor program. The commission has plans to push ahead with the development of different types of converters and advanced breeder reactors in cooperation with private industry under a variety of arrangements. Without special inducements, enough private investment may not be forthcoming to make use of all the newly developing technological possibilities. Research on civilian uses of atomic energy—physical as well as biological and medical research—are projected as increasing steadily. Of the established civilian uses, it is expected that the production and marketing of isotopes will be transferred to private enterprise. It is anticipated that the commission will be very active in research on the possible use of atomic energy in water desalinization projects and on the pos-

TABLE 19. Expenditures of Atomic Energy Commission, Administrative and Cash Budgets, 1963, 1966, 1968, and 1973

(In billions of current dollars for fiscal years)

Fiscal year	Present policy projection[a]	As a percentage of GNP[b]	Arms reduction alternative[c]	As a percentage of GNP
Actual				
1963	2.8	0.5%		
Proposed				
1966	2.5	0.4		
Projected				
1968	2.7	[d]	2.6	0.3%
1973	3.2	0.3	3.0	0.3

[a] The assumptions used for projections under "present policy" are roughly comparable to those of Model I and Model II-A1.
[b] Projected GNP for Model II was used to calculate this percentage.
[c] The assumptions used for projections under "arms reduction" are closest to Model II-A2 and Model II-B.
[d] The percentage is 0.35.

sible use of nuclear explosions for civilian excavation and construction (of which a sea-level canal between the Atlantic and Pacific Oceans is a possibility).

While the AEC will undoubtedly play a role in any future program dealing with high-energy physics, the bulk of such expenditures is projected for the education and research functional category.

International Affairs and Finance

This functional category includes all federal activities concerned with the conduct of foreign affairs—international economic and financial programs as well as foreign information and education activities. For our purposes, we have included projections for

TABLE 20. Model I and Model II: Federal Expenditures for International Affairs and Finance, Administrative and Cash Budgets, 1963, 1966, 1968, and 1973

(In billions of current dollars for fiscal years)

Item	Actual 1963	Pro-posed 1966	Projected 1968			Projected 1973		
			Model I	Model II-A	Model II-B	Model I	Model II-A	Model II-B
Department of State[a]	0.4	0.4	0.5	0.5	0.5	0.6	0.7	0.7
International police force	—	—	—	0.2	0.8	—	1.0	2.3
Foreign economic assistance[b]	2.2	2.2	2.5	2.6	3.2	2.6	4.0	5.5
Export-Import Bank[c]	−0.4	−0.5	−0.1	—	0.2	—	0.3	0.5
U. S. Information Agency	0.2	0.2	0.2	0.3	0.4	0.4	0.4	0.6
Food-for-Peace program[d]	1.8	1.8	1.7	1.8	1.8	1.9	2.0	2.0
Other[e]	—	—	—	0.1	0.1	—	0.1	0.2
Total, administrative budget	4.2	4.0	4.8	5.5	7.0	5.5	8.5	11.8
Total, cash budget[f]	3.8	4.2	4.8	5.5	7.0	5.5	8.5	11.8
Total, cash budget, as a percentage of GNP	0.7	0.6	0.65	0.7	0.9	0.5	0.8	1.2

Note: Details may not add to totals due to rounding.
[a] Includes, among other expenditures, memberships in and contributions to international organizations, except those listed separately in this table.
[b] Includes Agency for International Development, Peace Corps, and subscriptions to international financial institutions.
[c] Minus figures indicate an excess of sales of loans to private buyers from the Export-Import Bank portfolio and other receipts over and above the Bank's expenditures.
[d] Includes other agricultural relief programs.
[e] Includes the Arms Control and Disarmament Agency.
[f] Intragovernmental transactions and adjustments for net cash issuances and withdrawals by international financial institutions follow an irregular pattern, and their influence has been treated as negligible when projecting actual payments to the public. Trust fund expenditures under this functional classification are usually small and likely to become insignificant, as the largest item—the Foreign Claims Settlement Commission—will decline in importance.

the Department of State; foreign economic assistance, including the Agency for International Development, the Peace Corps, and the Export-Import Bank; and the United States Information Agency. In addition, Table 20 gives projections for the Food-for-Peace and famine relief programs of the Department of Agriculture and a very small residual amount for several other agencies included in this category.

Department of State

The expenditures of the Department of State fall into three major categories. The most important of these, the administration of foreign affairs, includes salaries and expenses, the acquisition and maintenance of buildings abroad, and several minor items. In fiscal 1965, expenditures in this category will account for about 50 percent of total expenditures and must be expected to increase steadily in keeping with the role of the United States in world affairs and the increasing complexity of international relations. Memberships and contributions to international organizations, including the United Nations, will undoubtedly continue as a major item of expenditure and will probably show moderate though irregular increases.

Models II-A and II-B include, as an additional item, substantial sums for contributions to a greatly enlarged international police force. This is true particularly of Model II-B (the arms reduction model), since an enlarged United Nations force would have to accompany any global arms reduction program.

Educational exchange programs, the third major category of expenditures, are projected to rise beyond current levels. Again this is true particularly of the Model II-B estimates, because of their importance in contributing to international understanding.

Funds Appropriated to the President

The great bulk of American nonmilitary foreign aid expenditures falls in this category, including all the far-flung activities of the Agency for International Development, investments in and subscriptions to international financial institutions, and Peace Corps expenditures.

DEVELOPMENT LOANS. Model I shows our projection of expenditures under current policies. Two items that are expected to account for considerably increased expenditures are loans under the Alliance for Progress in Latin America and funds for the Development Loan Revolving Fund. The latter emphasize the long-run development of productive capacity and carry an interest rate of only 0.75 percent. Most assistance to India is in this category, as is aid to many other countries. The loans under the Alliance for Progress are similar in character, and it is anticipated that these two loan funds will constitute major channels of American aid.

CONTRIBUTIONS TO INTERNATIONAL ORGANIZATIONS. Such contributions are assumed to increase somewhat, particularly because they include U.N. technical assistance, the U.N. Children's Fund, and many special programs, support for which is defended on humanitarian grounds. Provision is also included for a somewhat larger contingencies fund to provide the President with flexibility in meeting unforeseen emergencies and opportunities in foreign affairs.

International financial institutions, such as the International Development Association and the International Monetary Fund, will continue to be supported, although it is difficult to project this on a year-by-year basis since in most instances contributions are made at irregular intervals.

Models II-A and II-B are designed to take account of possible new developments in the international sector. Both models, but particularly Model II-B, project increased expenditures. The Alliance for Progress programs are viewed as one of the principal avenues of expansion, and Model II-B assumes that aid to Latin America will reach Marshall Plan dimensions, with disbursements in excess of $20 billion during the period under discussion. Substantial increases are also assumed for development grants and loans to underdeveloped countries outside Latin America, particularly in connection with new American efforts in Africa and in support of the Fourth Five-Year Plan of India, beginning in 1966.

Increased aid channeled through the U.N. and other international bodies, such as the International Development Association, are also regarded as probable.

Altogether, in the high-expenditure Model II-B all international programs would exceed the level of 1 percent of GNP regarded as desirable by the United Nations.

THE PEACE CORPS. This has been one of the outstanding successes among American international programs. Its continued further expansion to a 1973 level of 30,000 volunteers under Model I and to 60,000 in Model II-B has been projected.

EXPORT-IMPORT BANK. During the period 1963-65, the Export-Import Bank's receipts from operations and its sale of loan assets from its portfolio have exceeded expenditures. Thus the Bank's operations have shown a net surplus in the administrative budget. This cannot be expected to continue indefinitely, if only because the inventory of desirable loans is bound to be very low after fiscal 1965. We have also been guided by expectations of continued expansion in world trade and in United States exports. Therefore, our models assume a "neutral" budget position for the Bank in 1968 and project that thereafter additional funds for its operations will be required, reaching $0.5 billion in 1973.

FOOD-FOR-PEACE. Through the Food-for-Peace program, United States agricultural surplus foods are made available to help feed hungry people and contribute to economic development abroad. Under Public Law 480, most of such surplus commodities are sold partly for inconvertible currencies and to a smaller extent on long-term credit for dollars, or they are given away as grants. Expenditures under this and an older famine relief program are expected to remain rather stable at around $2 billion in all our models, but they will continue to be an important factor in the United States' international posture.

UNITED STATES INFORMATION AGENCY. Expenditures for USIA have been projected on an increasing scale, both in Model I and in Models II-A and II-B. The agency is charged with disseminating to other countries information about the United States and its cultural objectives and is certain to require substantial and increasing program funds for radio, television, motion pictures, and other media. The contest for influence and understanding must be expected to continue in a world that is becoming increasingly literate and aware.

UNITED STATES ARMS CONTROL AND DISARMAMENT AGENCY. While present expenditures of this agency are small, they could assume greater importance, particularly in connection with a policy of arms reduction. This is reflected in our projection for Model II-B.

Space Research and Technology

All federal activities in the field of space research and technology are the responsibility of the National Aeronautics and Space Administration. Any projection of the NASA budget for ten years must be subject to a wide margin of error. The agency is relatively new and is engaged in research and development in uncharted fields. (See Table 21.)

Cost estimates for these pioneering projects are understandably unreliable. The goals of the agency for the ten-year period and the rate at which they will be pursued are not explicit, except, of

TABLE 21. Model I and Model II: Federal Expenditures for Space Research and Technology under Reduced and Stepped-up Programs, Cash Budget, 1963, 1966, 1968, and 1973

(In billions of current dollars for fiscal years)

Item	Actual 1963	Proposed 1966	Projected 1968	Projected 1973
Model I:				
Actual, proposed, and projected expenditures	2.6	5.1	6.0	6.0
As a percentage of GNP	0.5	0.7	0.8	0.7
Model II-A (Low Model):				
Projected expenditures			4.0	4.0
As a percentage of GNP			0.5	0.4
Model II-B (High Model):				
Projected expenditures			7.0	6.5
As a percentage of GNP			0.9	0.6

course, for the manned lunar landing. The determination of the agency's budget over the next ten years is inextricably bound up with other issues: international relations, domestic politics, and economic growth. Also an important determinant will be NASA's record of success or failure during the period, because successes will undoubtedly open up new vistas for the entire space field, while failures may result either in an increased effort or in disillusionment.

NASA Programs

The National Aeronautics and Space Administration conducts six major types of programs.

THE MANNED SPACE FLIGHT PROGRAM. This program accounts for about two-thirds of NASA's total estimated 1965 expenditures and includes funds for developing the Gemini and Apollo spacecraft and the launch vehicles for their respective missions. Project Gemini is scheduled to undertake prolonged earth orbits and to practice space rendezvous and docking techniques to be used later in the Apollo program. Project Apollo will make progress toward putting a three-man spacecraft in orbit around the moon for the lunar landing.

THE SPACE APPLICATIONS PROGRAM. This covers work on the weather and communications satellites and the dissemination of technological information to industry. An effort will be made to encourage commercial applications of ideas and inventions developed under the NASA program.

UNMANNED INVESTIGATIONS IN SPACE. About 14 percent of NASA's estimated 1965 expenditures will be for unmanned investigations in space. These include funds for unmanned space flight missions to gather basic scientific data and the development of the related launch vehicles. The principal programs in this category are projects Ranger and Surveyor for lunar exploration, Mariner and Voyager for studies of Mars and Venus, and Pioneer for a series of interplanetary probes.

SPACE RESEARCH AND DEVELOPMENT. This program absorbed about 10 percent of NASA's estimated 1965 expenditures. Under it the technology required to develop and operate space vehicle systems and related equipment and components is advanced. Research and development are related to technical disciplines and problem areas of space flight: space environment effects, aerothermodynamics, guidance and control systems, and re-entry phenomena. It is probable that most of these studies directly support the moon programs. Also work on propulsion and space power systems, which will provide the key to future space vehicles and potential missions, is carried on in this activity.

SUPPORTING OPERATIONS. These include tracking and data acquisition for space flights, and training and research grants to universities.

AIRCRAFT TECHNOLOGY. This program covers work on the supersonic transport (for the Federal Aviation Agency) and other projects.

Projections

Model I shows the likely progress of projects according to existing policies, with a manned lunar landing achieved by fiscal 1971 and followed by the establishment of a lunar base and preparations for other space projects.

Model II shows two alternatives: Model II-A is a reduced program, stretching out the time of the lunar landing to 1973, with only small expenditures for other programs. Model II-B is a stepped-up version with increased expenditures, continuing for the period after the lunar landing is achieved. Model II-B would also finance a significant level of nonlunar activities and signify an energetic pursuit of the interplanetary programs.

CHAPTER VIII

Economic Development and Education

THIS CHAPTER DISCUSSES expenditures that are concerned primarily with the support of economic development in the United States, defined in a broad sense. They include the functional categories of Natural Resources, Commerce and Transportation, and Education and Research, but the consideration of research activities in this sense is limited to the National Science Foundation and new research programs that may be expected to become operational during the period covered by the study. Other research activities of the federal government are treated within the applicable functional categories. Health research and defense-connected research are prominent examples.

The principal departments and agencies covered in this chapter are the Department of the Interior, the Corps of Engineers of the Department of Defense, the Forest Service of the Department of Agriculture, the Department of Commerce, the Office of Education of the Department of Health, Education, and Welfare, the Post Office, the National Science Foundation, and a host of smaller agencies. Among the latter are the Tennessee Valley Authority, the Coast Guard of the Department of the Treasury, the Federal Avia-

104   Federal Budget Projections

TABLE 22. Model I and Model II: Federal Expenditures for Natural Resources, Administrative and Cash Budgets, 1963, 1966, 1968, and 1973

(In billions of current dollars for fiscal years)

Agency	Actual 1963	Proposed 1966	Projected 1968			Projected 1973		
			Model I	Model II-A	Model II-B	Model I	Model II-A	Model II-B
Department of the Interior	0.9	1.0	1.4	1.5	1.7	1.8	2.0	2.3
Corps of Engineers	1.1	1.2	1.3	1.4	1.5	1.5	1.7	1.9
Forest Service	0.3	0.3	0.4	0.5	0.5	0.4	0.5	0.6
Other (mainly Tennessee Valley Authority)	0.1	0.1	0.1	0.1	0.1	0.1	0.1	0.1
Total, administrative budget	2.4	2.7	3.2	3.5	3.8	3.8	4.3	4.9
Total, cash budget[a]	2.5	2.9	3.3	3.6	3.9	3.9	4.4	5.0
Total, cash budget, as a percentage of GNP	0.4	0.4	0.4	0.5	0.5	0.4	0.4	0.5

Note: Details may not add to totals due to rounding.
[a] Includes Indian Tribal Trust Funds.

tion Agency, the Small Business Administration, and all agencies devoted to the regulation of business and banking.

Natural Resources

Federal government activities falling under the natural resources function include the bulk of the services provided by the Department of the Interior, the civil functions of the Department of Defense performed through the Corps of Engineers, the Forest Service of the Department of Agriculture, the Tennessee Valley Authority, and a few minor activities of other agencies.[1] (See Table 22.)

Department of the Interior

The principal activities of the Interior Department may be grouped under four separate major sections, in addition to its expenditures for the Secretary's offices and general administration.

[1] The following activities are classified under other functional categories: Indian education services of the Department of the Interior are under Education; the Office of Territories of the Department of the Interior is under General Government; the administration of the Ryukyu Islands and the Panama Canal by the Department of Defense is under General Government.

PUBLIC LAND MANAGEMENT. This is the most important division, accounting for almost one-half of the departmental budget. Its most prominent bureaus are: Land Management, Indian Affairs, the National Park Service, and the Bureau of Outdoor Recreation. In our projections we have assumed increases for each of these, particularly the latter three.[2] Since recreation is generally regarded as a "growth activity" and the needs for it are continually increasing, the reasons for these choices are clear. In Model I almost $700 million of expenditures have been projected for these purposes, while in Model II-B they are projected to reach almost the $1 billion level.

MINERAL RESOURCES. Expansion in this field has been more limited. For the future, considerable expansion has been assumed for the Geological Survey, as well as some increases in expenditures for the Bureau of Mines.

FISH AND WILDLIFE SERVICE. These expenditures are assumed to show appreciable increases under Model I and even greater ones under Models II-A and II-B. These are largely for the steadily expanding recreational activities, with some additions also for commercial fisheries.

WATER AND POWER DEVELOPMENT. Expenditures for water and power development were very hard to project. No large-scale shift in the public-private power relationship was assumed in any model. The most important activities in this field are performed by the Bureau of Reclamation, and a considerable expansion of its activities is projected in all models. Additionally, Model II-B assumes that activities similar to those connected with the Upper Colorado River Basin Fund may be extended to other areas.[3] The Bureau of Reclamation generates substantial revenues, which are plowed back into its operations, and these too are assumed to increase. The Office of Saline Water and the Bonneville Power Administration are others with significant expenditures. Increased expenditures by

[2] Based on reports of the Outdoor Recreation Resources Review Commission.
[3] Based in part on Nathaniel Wollman, *A Preliminary Report on the Supply of and Demand for Water in the United States as Estimated for 1980 and 2000,* Committee Print No. 32 of the Senate Select Committee on National Water Resources (August 1960).

the Office of Saline Water are projected, particularly in Models II-A and II-B, in connection with the water desalinization program, which is beginning to show promising results. It must be remembered, however, that other agencies are also participating in this program.

In a study of this nature it is difficult to be firm about departmental responsibilities for new programs or for present programs that are greatly expanded. For example, the Department of the Interior may well have a role in the increasingly important area of water pollution prevention and control. This is at present the responsibility of the Public Health Service and is considered in that agency's expenditures in our projections.

Department of Defense (Corps of Engineers)

The activities of the Corps of Engineers are of considerable scope and spread over the entire map of the United States. Its most important expenditures are for numerous new construction projects, as well as large amounts for the operation and maintenance of its existing facilities. There is also a revolving fund for civil works functions. Construction expenditures are by far the most important and include navigation projects, flood control projects, and such multiple-purpose projects as those for power development. Many undertakings of the Corps have been criticized as "pork barrel" expenditures. While there is certainly a political aspect to these programs, this should not obscure the fact that most of its work has been extremely useful. The Corps' flood control work along the Mississippi and along many other rivers, its many navigation projects throughout the United States and in Puerto Rico, and its multiple-purpose projects have been of immeasurable benefit to the many communities concerned.

Our projections assume increases in activities and expenditures for these purposes throughout the period under study, since the development of natural resources, and the part played in it by the Corps of Engineers, seem assured of steady support in Congress as well as by the general public. Model II-B (and to a more limited extent Model II-A) assumes additional expenditures, particularly for work on storage dams for low-waterflow augmentation, to combat water pollution, and for other construction work.

Department of Agriculture (Forest Service)

A slow but steady expansion of expenditures for this service is anticipated. The importance of preserving America's forest resources is likely to receive increasing emphasis in coming years. Certainly expenditures for forest protection and utilization, for forest roads and trails, and for the development of national forests will continue to be regarded as essential. This is reflected in our projections.[4]

Tennessee Valley Authority

We have assumed that TVA's program expenditures will be met increasingly from proceeds from power operations and nonpower activities and commercial borrowings, and that expenditures from appropriations, which are a net charge on the federal budget, will not increase.

Commerce and Transportation

This functional sector comprises the Department of Commerce, the Post Office, the Federal Aviation Agency, the Civil Aeronautics Board, the Coast Guard, and the Accelerated Public Works Program (for which funds are appropriated to the President). In addition, the Small Business Administration and a host of business regulatory agencies are included here.[5] Trust fund expenditures include the mammoth Highway Trust Fund, which accounts for more than half the expenditures in this entire functional classification, and the surplus of receipts (mainly from premiums in excess of expenditures) of the Federal Deposit Insurance Corporation. This surplus is applied to reduce consolidated cash budget expenditures for this classification. (See Table 23.)

---

[4] Based on adaptations of Charles H. Stoddard, "Estimates of Needs," *Journal of Forestry* (July 1958). See also Hans H. Landsberg, Joseph L. Fisher, and Leonard L. Fischman, *Resources in America's Future: Patterns of Requirements and Availabilities, 1960-2000* (Johns Hopkins Press for Resources for the Future, Inc., 1963).

[5] The Federal Communications Commission, Federal Maritime Commission, Interstate Commerce Commission, and Securities and Exchange Commission; also some minor agencies and the Antitrust Division of the Department of Justice.

TABLE 23. Model I and Model II: Federal Expenditures for Commerce and Transportation[a], Administrative and Cash Budgets, 1963, 1966, 1968, and 1973

(In billions of current dollars for fiscal years)

Agency	Actual 1963	Pro-posed 1966	Projected 1968			Projected 1973		
			Model I	Model II-A	Model II-B	Model I	Model II-A	Model II-B
Department of Commerce[b]	0.7	0.8	1.4	1.6	1.8	2.0	2.3	2.6
Federal Aviation Agency	0.7	0.8	1.2	1.4	1.6	1.5	1.9	2.2
Post Office Department	0.8	0.7	0.7	0.7	0.7	1.0	1.0	0.5[d]
Coast Guard, Civil Aeronautics Board, Small Business Administration, Accelerated Public Works, etc.	0.6	0.6	0.7	1.0	1.1	0.8	1.3	1.6
Total, administrative budget	2.8	2.8	4.0	4.7	5.2	5.3	6.5	6.9
Highway Trust Fund[c]	3.0	3.9	4.4	4.4	4.4	5.5	5.5	6.5
Other trust funds, less surplus of Federal Deposit Insurance Corporation and intergovernmental transfers	0.0	−0.2	−0.3	−0.4	−0.4	−0.4	−0.5	−0.5
Total, cash budget	5.8	6.5	8.1	8.7	9.2	10.4	11.5	12.9
Total, cash budget, as a percentage of GNP	1.0	1.0	1.1	1.1	1.2	1.1	1.1	1.3

Note: Details may not add to totals due to rounding.
a Excludes those activities of the listed agencies that are classified functionally under other headings.
b Models II-A and II-B imply a reduction in the expenditures for the Maritime Commission and increases in others, including ARA.
c Model II-B includes a one-cent gasoline tax increase in 1970 and continuation of the higher rate through fiscal 1973. The gasoline tax is scheduled to drop to 1.5 cents a gallon on October 1, 1972. However, Models I and II-A assume that the tax will be continued at the existing rates.
d Assumes an increase in postal rates.

The Department of Commerce

The Department of Commerce comprises a multiplicity of diverse operations, all of which are designed to assist business. Apart from general administration, these may be grouped under the headings of economic development, science and technology, and transportation.

Under economic development are the two larger bureaus, the Bureau of the Census and the Area Redevelopment Administration, in addition to a number of important smaller offices.[6] Some of these smaller offices, notably the Office of Business Economics and, to a lesser extent, the Business and Defense Services Administration, are responsible for a considerable portion of the economic research carried out by the federal government. Substantial increases in the present modest appropriations for these purposes are projected. The same applies to the smaller bureaus connected with various aspects of world trade and travel.

The Bureau of the Census is the main "statistics factory" of the federal government. It has grown steadily in stature and importance, and this trend is expected to continue. Projections for the Bureau must take account of the bulge in expenditures made necessary by the decennial censuses of population and the minor temporary increases associated with the various censuses of agriculture, manufacturing, distribution, and transportation. The trend in Bureau of the Census expenditures may be characterized as "irregularly upward."

The Area Redevelopment Administration is a special case. The problem of how to attract new firms to communities in economically distressed areas will continue to be acute even in periods of general prosperity. This agency's attempts to resuscitate depressed areas by attracting new industry will require increasing expenditures, particularly if its responsibilities are further enlarged (Models II-A and II-B). Some of these activities need not involve budget expenditures, as, for example, the proposed federal guarantees of working capital loans for industrial projects. The Appalachia program is now the responsibility of an independent commission, and a number of special programs for other problem areas may be launched over a period of years.

Another field with strong expansionary potential is that of science and technology.[7] All the science services of the Department of Commerce are important for the promotion of economic growth, and considerably increased expenditures for these activities have

[6] The Offices of Business Economics and Field Services, Business and Defense Services Administration, U.S. Travel Service, and various bureaus and offices dealing with international commerce.

[7] The Coast and Geodetic Survey, the Patent Office, the National Bureau of Standards, the Office of Technical Services, and the Weather Bureau. (The National Science Foundation is included under Education.)

been projected in all our models. Money spent for these purposes is likely to yield a very high return in benefits to the community.

In dollar terms, transportation is by far the most important of the Department's activities, and the Bureau of Public Roads undoubtedly has the greatest direct effect on the nation's economy. This is because the Bureau administers and controls the allocation of funds from the Highway Trust Fund, which pay for 90 percent of the new network of interstate superhighways and 50 percent of most other new highway construction. The fund is financed largely from a 4 cents a gallon levy on gasoline sales and thus can be projected with a fair degree of accuracy, given assumptions as to economic trends and consumer outlays. We have taken into account the increased highway user charges proposed by the administration for 1966 and have projected a continuation of all highway-related taxes through fiscal 1973 in all models. Model II-B assumes a 1 cent a gallon increase in the gasoline tax, starting in fiscal 1970. This assumption is made because the construction needs conservatively estimated by the Bureau of Public Roads will not be met unless federal aid is forthcoming. Some of the additional funds may be used to help states and localities pay for the greatly increased repair and maintenance expenses of the expanded road network. It is assumed that any shortfall in covering increased costs of constructing the Interstate Highway System will be borne by increased user charges imposed on truckers.

The Maritime Administration's two largest items of expenditure are operating-differential subsidies for American-flag shipping and construction subsidies for vessels built in American yards. They are defended largely on the grounds of national security. It is assumed that total expenditures of the Maritime Administration will continue at the same level. If any "savings" in subsidy costs are realized, they may well be used to stimulate expenditures on experimental vessels powered by atomic energy.

The Commerce Department's efforts in transportation research will undoubtedly expand. An example is its study of transportation problems in the Northeast Corridor of the United States.[8]

[8] Transportation research is carried on also by the Housing and Home Finance Agency.

Treasury Department (Coast Guard)

It has been assumed that expenditures for the Coast Guard will continue on a fairly steady level, with some increases in pay and allowances of personnel and with a program of capital outlays for replacing and modernizing the fleet to keep it in top operating condition.

Post Office Department

Almost since its inception, controversy has raged over the question whether the Post Office should be run as a business, covering its expenses fully, or as an essential public service. In practice, compromises of various kinds have been adopted to bridge the gap between the two conceptions, such as labeling certain expenditures "Public Service Expenditures." Our projections have assumed an increase of 35 percent in the volume of mail for the ten-year period 1964-73. Productivity is expected to show substantial gains, largely because of the more rapid introduction of automation into the system. Over-all employment increases are held down to about 1 percent annually.

Our projections for Models I and II-A assume that the present "compromise" arrangements will continue and that there will be no further general increase in postal rates. On the other hand, Model II-B assumes that a general increase in postal rates will be sanctioned to take effect in fiscal 1970 and that the net charge on the administrative budget will be somewhat reduced. It is assumed that such an increase will allow more capital expenditures for increased efficiency and that automation in the Post Office will not be retarded because of fiscal considerations.

Federal Aviation Agency

FAA publishes medium-term (five-year) projections intended to show the anticipated levels of expenditures for its various functions. These projections have had to be revised from time to time in the past, an experience supporting our suggestion that all such projections have to be brought up to date periodically. In our models, it has been assumed that the federal government will continue to bear the costs of air navigation and traffic control facilities and equipment, and that the grants-in-aid program for airports will continue at about the present level. Research and development funds have been projected to increase. Subsidies for the supersonic airliner were a difficult problem in view of the uncertain aspects of the program. It has been assumed that expenditures will exceed $1 billion and will continue after the end of fiscal 1973. Model II-B assumes that the government contribution to meet the costs of the supersonic airliner will be stepped up to 95 percent and that development will be at a faster rate. It also assumes some federal contributions for a civilian adaptation of the giant cargo and passenger transport plane being developed by the Air Force as a troop carrier.

Miscellaneous Agencies

Expenditures of the Civil Aeronautics Board are bound to increase with expanding air traffic. The largest portion by far of the Board's costs consists of payments to regional and feeder airlines, and these are likely to continue.

Small Business Administration expenditures are in large part financed by means of a revolving fund, to which interest, loan repayments, and sales of loans to private investors are credited. These funds can then be used to make new loans without creating a net charge on either the administrative or the cash budget. Such internally financed expenditures have constituted about two-thirds of all agency expenditures during the past few years, and they are expected to provide a sizable surplus in fiscal 1966. However, our projections treat 1966 as a special case and assume a continuation of recent trends in Models I and II-A, with somewhat stepped up expenditures for Model II-B, particularly to provide further resources for improved operations of private Small Business Investment Corporations and for the "very small loans" program.

Budgetary expenditures of the business regulatory agencies have been projected as increasing in line with general economic trends.

Expenditures for Accelerated Public Works are being phased out and have been disregarded in our Models I and II-A. For II-B, however, some such program, envisaged rather as a permanent additional grant program to promote expenditures for needed public works at the local level, has been assumed.

Since we assume generally prosperous conditions, the Federal Deposit Insurance Corporation (the trust fund that insures bank deposits) has been projected as showing consistent net surpluses, gradually building up to around $350 million annually. The surplus serves to reduce the net expenditure side of the consolidated cash budget for this functional classification.

Education and Research[9]

Substantial federal expenditures for education and research are of relatively recent origin. Therefore, in making projections, we could not be guided by past experience. Today the overwhelming importance of providing the best possible educational opportunities for all Americans has become clear to almost everyone. It is realized that the continued leadership of the United States in the field of human progress is dependent on success in achieving this goal. The necessary expenditures are so large that the increasing involvement of the federal government in this area has become essential, and our projections reflect this. (See Table 24.)

A large number of agencies are concerned with some aspect of educational expenditures. However, the bulk of all such outlays is made by the Office of Education in the Department of Health, Education, and Welfare. Other important expenditures in this functional category are those of the College Housing program of the Housing and Home Finance Agency, the Department of Interior's educational services on Indian reservations, and such special institutions as the Library of Congress, the Smithsonian Institution, Howard University, and Gallaudet College.

The Office of Education is the principal agency responsible for assistance given to education by the federal government. It operates almost exclusively as a grant-giving and administering agency, the actual expenditure of funds being left to the individual states or educational institutions. Specific grants cover the promotion and further development of vocational education, and assistance to land-grant colleges. Grants are also given for foreign language training, for library services (mostly in rural areas), for training teachers of the handicapped, and for various educational research programs. In addition the Office administers all payments to local school districts under the impacted areas program, under which payments are

[9] Activities in this category include National Science Foundation and research programs that have not been classified elsewhere.

Federal Budget Projections

TABLE 24. Model I and Model II: Federal Expenditures for Education and Research, Administrative and Cash Budgets, 1963, 1966, 1968, and 1973

(In billions of current dollars for fiscal years)

Agency	Actual 1963	Pro- posed 1966	Projected 1968			Projected 1973		
			Model I	Model II-A	Model II-B	Model I	Model II-A	Model II-B
Assistance to elementary and secondary education	0.4	1.0	1.8	2.0	2.1	3.0	3.5	4.2
Assistance to higher education[a]	0.4	0.8	1.2	1.4	1.7	3.0	3.5	5.1
Vocational education and other aids[b]	0.2	0.5	0.7	0.7	0.7	1.0	1.1	1.2
National Science Foundation	0.2	0.4	0.5	0.5	0.6	0.7	0.9	1.1
New research programs	—	—	0.1	0.2	0.2	0.3	0.5	0.9
Total, administrative budget[c]	1.2	2.7	4.3	4.8	5.3	8.0	9.5	12.5
Total, administrative and cash budgets, as a percentage of GNP	0.2	0.4	0.6	0.6	0.7	0.9	0.95	1.25

[a] Includes college housing loan program.

[b] Includes other defense education assistance, Indian education services, Library of Congress, Smithsonian Institution, grants for public libraries, and others.

[c] For 1966, expenditures in the cash budget were $2.6 billion. For 1968 and 1973, the difference between the administrative and cash budgets are assumed to be negligible.

made for children whose parents live on federal property or work for the federal government. It is also responsible for administering activities under the National Defense Education Act.

Future federal expenditures to aid education will be governed by two principal determinants: the growth of the school- and college-age population and the continuing improvement in the operation of all educational services.

Assistance to Elementary and Secondary Education

Federal aid to elementary and secondary education has in the past been confined to assistance under the National Defense Education Act, which was broadened in 1964 to include additional subjects, and to assistance to schools in federally impacted areas. Expenditures in these categories for fiscal 1966 are scheduled at $472 million, nearly three-quarters of which is for the impacted areas program. This represents only slightly more than 2 percent of total state and local expenditures for these purposes. The administration has thus proposed additional programs for elementary and secondary education, with special emphasis on helping children in low-income areas and including those attending private and parochial schools. Whereas only $500 million is expected to be spent in fiscal 1966, new obligational authority requested for that year exceeds $1.25 billion. The program is virtually certain to be expanded considerably in future years, and this is reflected in our models.

When judging such assistance on a "needs" basis, it should be borne in mind that during the decade 1964-73 the number of children in age groups attending elementary and secondary schools will increase by about 20 percent, which is only slightly higher than the expected growth in the general population. From this point of view, and given our assumptions of reasonably full employment, it should be possible to finance the growing needs from state and local tax sources, especially since the growth rate in the number of children in these age groups will be lower than it was during the 1950's.

However, average figures conceal grave local deficiencies which cannot be overcome without substantial outside assistance; if a fairly rapid general lifting of standards is desired, effective federal help will be indispensable. There are obvious deficiencies in the area of preschool education, which is increasingly recognized as being of extreme importance for the future mental development of the child. Only two-thirds of all children scheduled to begin first grade the following year are enrolled in kindergarten classes. Another deficiency is at the upper end of the scale, where the number of dropouts in the last two years of high school has occasioned increasing concern.

For these reasons, the administration proposals focus on the problems of the poorer school districts, where these deficiencies are most apparent. Our projections for 1973 show total federal assistance, including the proposed new programs, at nearly $3 billion in Model I, which would probably be just over 10 percent of all expenditures for this purpose (private, federal, state, and local). Larger amounts are projected in the other models. Model II-B assumes a professional-pupil ratio of fifty to one thousand and involves considerably more federal assistance. In Model II-A federal expenditures for this purpose fall somewhere between those in Models I and II-B.

Assistance to Higher Education

Enrollment pressures for higher education will become exceedingly serious during the next ten years; some estimates by the Office of Education envisage a 90 percent increase in enrollment between 1962 and 1973.[10] With only an 18 percent rise in the population as a whole, obviously the community must assume a far greater burden. In 1961-62 all levels of government provided more than 50 percent of all funds for higher education, the federal share being 25.6 percent of the total.[11] In fiscal 1966 net federal expenditures for this purpose are approaching $800 million, but total expenditures in this field have risen so much that the federal share is probably not much higher than it was in 1957. Total outlays for higher education are bound to rise even more than the enrollment projections indicate. Estimates that the United States may be spending about 1.75 percent of GNP on higher education by 1973 (exclusive of construction) do not seem excessive. This contrasts with just less than 1 percent spent for this purpose in 1962-63 and indicates the magnitude of the task facing the country's institutions of higher learning during the next ten years. Because of the federal government's role in this task, great expenditure increases are projected for the future in all our models.

Federally insured long-term college housing loans at low rates of interest have been of great importance in making possible physical expansion of the nation's institutions of higher learning. This program will continue to be of great significance, though its net impact on the federal budget may not indicate its full influence because some of the loans may be sold to private investors. The separate program to help build classrooms, libraries, and laboratories is only now, in 1965, beginning to get into full swing, and our estimates include greatly increased amounts for these purposes for future years.

On the college level, National Defense Education Act assistance has been channeled into student loans, fellowships, and programs

[10] U.S. Office of Education, Department of Health, Education, and Welfare, *Projections of Educational Statistics to 1973-74* (U.S. Government Printing Office, 1964).

[11] U.S. Office of Education, *Preliminary Report of Financial Statistics of Institutions of Higher Education, 1961-62*, Circular No. 52008 (Washington, D.C., July 1963).

aiding teacher training in various fields. Since it is the administration's avowed aim to make college education possible for all deserving students from lower income groups, great increases in the cost of these programs have been assumed for all our models. This is so particularly for Model II-B, which envisages a great increase in educational services provided by junior colleges and community colleges, so that by the end of the period the completion of a two-year college course or an equivalent technical course will be as common as the completion of a high school education was as recently as the late 1940's. At that time only about 45 percent of all young people who had entered fifth grade continued their education long enough to graduate from high school. Another field where there are educational needs that community colleges can meet is that of adult education. Both supplemental and remedial courses are of value.

Vocational Education and Other Programs

Very large increases are projected for vocational education, particularly in connection with the anti-poverty program and also to provide an avenue of advancement for many young people who will never be academically oriented. The need for competent technicians has never been greater, and a thorough upgrading of vocational instruction would help meet the demand for an increasingly skilled labor force.

It is assumed that the newly enlarged public library assistance program will grow in importance, and steadily increasing appropriations are assumed for the Library of Congress and the Smithsonian Institution. The remaining educational expenditures, for Indian educational programs as well as for the special institutions mentioned above, will also show a steadily rising trend although over-all figures are likely to remain modest for these purposes.

Research (National Science Foundation and New Programs Not Elsewhere Classified)

Many federal agencies are involved in research and development programs. In dollar terms, most important by far are the expenditures of the Department of Defense, with $6.9 billion scheduled for this purpose in fiscal 1966, followed by the National Aeronautics and Space Administration ($5.1 billion), and the Atomic Energy Commission ($1.6 billion). Of the purely civilian agencies, the Department of Health, Education, and Welfare ranks first with expenditures approaching $1 billion. Significant expenditures will also be incurred by the Departments of Agriculture, Commerce, and Interior, and the Federal Aviation Agency and National Science Foundation. Nearly two-thirds of the total federal expenditures for research and development of about $15 billion relate to development, and almost all of this is spent by the Department of Defense, NASA, and the AEC. Of the remaining $5 billion, nearly $3 billion is for applied research, and the same three agencies account for about 70 percent of this, with HEW, Agriculture, and the National Science Foundation spending most of the remainder. Even for basic research, NASA, Defense, and the AEC between them will spend two-thirds of the total, with other significant amounts being spent only by HEW, the National Science Foundation, and the Department of Agriculture. NASA, Defense, and AEC also account for more than 75 percent of all amounts spent for research and development facilities. HEW concentrates on medical and health-related research. Expenditures for the atmospheric sciences are still largely in the hands of Defense and NASA; those for oceanography involve mostly Defense, the National Science Foundation, Interior, and Commerce; and water research is carried on mostly by Interior, HEW, and Agriculture.

Our projections of research and development expenditures have been integrated with projections of agency responsibility in their particular fields, so that only the National Science Foundation and future research projects not elsewhere classified are treated in this category. The Foundation performs a vital role in support of science education and basic research, and its expenditures have been rising continually for a number of years. While the same rate of expansion cannot be maintained indefinitely, our projection assumes further increases, in both the research grant and the science fellowship programs. In the past, research grants have been confined largely to the top universities that have shown outstanding capabilities in certain fields. However, these grants—which are an effective means of federal support for higher education—are expected to be more widely spread in the future in order to create such capabilities on a broader base. All activities of the NSF are expected to share in this progress, with special emphasis on its assistance for basic research, specialized research facilities, and grants for institutional science programs. With the ever-increasing complexities and greater specialization of modern research, its needs will become constantly more important, and this will mean large increases in the National Science Foundation's activities devoted to these purposes. The Foundation's responsibilities in the field of science education are of special importance in this connection. Again some research resources may be switched from the defense and space areas to general civilian purposes, and any such development will automatically increase the importance of the Foundation. Model II-B assumes that there will be an extensive special program in oceanography. It assumes also that a great many other promising areas of research will be supported by the National Science Foundation during the entire period, and NSF's total expenditures are projected to increase two and one-half times between fiscal 1966 and fiscal 1973 in our Model II-B, with more moderate increases for the other models.

Our projections for research also include amounts for unspecified new projects—ranging by 1973 from $0.2 billion in Model I to $1 billion in Model II-B. It is impossible to pinpoint this research in any detail. An obvious candidate is a greatly expanded oceanography program, which would really be an interdisciplinary venture in the truest sense, combining the talents of marine geologists, geographers, chemists, ichthyologists, marine botanists, and many others. Other examples are possible programs for research into solar energy, tidal water power (desalting of water has already been mentioned elsewhere), high-energy physics, meteorology, astronautics, and many others.

It is almost impossible to attach meaningful price tags to these ventures. For example, two different reports concerned with oceanography recommend expenditures of about $60 million[12] and $2.7 billion[13] for this purpose for the year 1969. Therefore, we preferred not to allocate specific amounts to individual research areas, but

[12] *Oceanography 1960-70*, Report of the Committee on Oceanography, National Academy of Sciences—National Research Council (1959).

[13] *A National Ocean Program*, Report of the National Security Industrial Association Ad Hoc Committee on Ocean Science and Technology (March 1964).

only to earmark an over-all sum for new research purposes for this model. We assume that many of these new research and development programs will be so organized that even a modest federal contribution will help to mobilize additional funds and talent from private resources. Then the total national effort for these purposes would far exceed the amounts we have projected for the federal budgets.

In this category belongs the proposed Foundation for the Humanities and the Arts, which figures in present administration proposals with a very modest starting budget. It is expected that this Foundation will also assist the social sciences. While support for such research will always remain small when compared with that for the physical sciences, the amounts devoted to this purpose must be expected to increase considerably over the years, and this is reflected in our estimates.

CHAPTER IX

Welfare Expenditures

THIS CATEGORY INCLUDES many of the most important nondefense activities of the federal government. Urgent needs exist in almost every field of expenditures described in this chapter. In large part, they are today being met from state and local funds, some with the help of federal grants-in-aid. The projections do not assume any significant shift of responsibility. However, we do assume a substantial shifting of federal funds toward increased grants-in-aid for many of these programs in all our models, particularly in Model II-B. This would be in addition to increases of direct federal expenditures for these purposes. In view of the increasing importance of expenditures in each of these fields, we are treating Health Services and Research, Labor, Economic Opportunity Programs, Social Insurance, and Welfare Services as separate functional categories. Expenditures for Housing and Community Development, for Agriculture, and for Veterans Services are also included under this general heading.

Health Services and Research

This category consists of the Public Health Service (including the National Institutes of Health), the Food and Drug Administration, and various health-connected programs of the Welfare

Administration.[1] All of these agencies are in the Department of Health, Education, and Welfare. (See Table 25.)

Food and Drug Administration

Expenditures for the Food and Drug Administration have been increasing rapidly during the last few years, largely because the public has finally realized the importance of the agency's responsibilities. These expenditures are bound to rise further as increasingly complex drugs and chemicals, as well as new methods of food processing, come to be used. However, the projected expenditures in this field, rising to $100 million by 1973, will always remain modest relative to those of other programs in this functional category.

Public Health Service

THE NATIONAL INSTITUTES OF HEALTH. The chief research arm of the Public Health Service is NIH.[2] Its spectacular growth since 1953 has been assisted by the sympathetic interest taken by influential members of Congress, supported by public opinion. One factor contributing to such widespread support is the fact that the largest part of NIH budget increases has gone not to finance its centralized operations but into research grants, chiefly to universities and research centers all over the country. All projections point to substantial further increases in health research expenditures as the number and remuneration of researchers and the amount spent on supporting staff and equipment all continue to rise. Models I and II-A assume that expenditures will triple between 1963 and 1973, and Model II-B assumes a further rise in expenditures to $2.5 billion. However, the rate of expenditure increases assumed in all models is well below that experienced during the previous decade.

All other activities of the Public Health Service will continue to receive increasing emphasis. It is expected that in the future great

[1] Grants for maternal and child welfare, the new program of grants for maternal and child health services, and the Children's Bureau. In addition, there are some foreign research outlays as well as expenditures for St. Elizabeths and Freedmen's Hospitals in Washington, D.C.

[2] The National Cancer and National Heart Institutes, as well as the Institutes for Mental Health, Allergy and Infectious Diseases, Dental Research, Arthritis and Metabolic Diseases, Neurological Diseases and Blindness, Child Health and Human Development, and General Medical Sciences—and several independent divisions—constitute the National Institutes of Health.

TABLE 25. Model I and Model II: Federal Expenditures for Health Services and Research, Administrative and Cash Budgets, 1963, 1966, 1968, and 1973

(In billions of current dollars for fiscal years)

Item	Actual 1963	Pro-posed 1966	Projected 1968			Projected 1973		
			Model I	Model II-A	Model II-B	Model I	Model II-A	Model II-B
National Institutes of Health	0.7	1.0	1.2	1.3	1.4	2.0	2.0	2.5
Hospital Construction[a]	0.2	0.2	0.4	0.5	0.6	0.7	1.0	1.2
Other Public Health services and other health activities[b]	0.4	1.0	1.2	1.4	1.7	2.0	2.5	3.5
Total, administrative and cash budgets	1.3	2.2	2.8	3.2	3.7	4.7	5.5	7.2
Total, administrative and cash budgets, as a percentage of GNP	0.2	0.3	0.4	0.4	0.5	0.5	0.5	0.7

[a] Includes nursing homes, health centers, etc.
[b] Includes Food and Drug Administration and child and maternal health activities.

importance will be attached to programs that will make research discoveries available as quickly as is compatible with safety to all Americans, and this will mean new responsibilities for the PHS. Its two major areas of activity are now Community Health and Environmental Health.

COMMUNITY HEALTH. This program is concerned with such vital services as worker accident prevention, chronic diseases and the health of the aged, and activities to combat communicable diseases, including such scourges as tuberculosis and venereal diseases. Considerable attention will continue to be devoted to the training of nurses and other hospital aides in order to relieve shortages in these fields.

The education assistance grants for training doctors and dentists and funds to support medical and dental schools will have to be increased considerably in order to meet the declared goal of increasing the number of doctors by 50 percent and of doubling the number of dentists during the next ten years. The 1966 budget marks a milestone in this direction. In this connection, it must be remembered that the United States is well down on the list of developed countries in the number of doctors per capita. Hospital construction activities under the Hill-Burton Act are also in this category. They have accounted for a steady stream of expenditures designed to spread hospital facilities more evenly throughout the nation, and in Model II-B we have assumed that these will increase in the future. With the continuing rise in the numbers of persons in the older age groups, which is bound to occur with advances in medical science, emphasis may be shifted toward the construction of more nursing home facilities under the Hill-Burton program.

Great benefits may be expected from the proposed new program for multipurpose regional medical complexes to provide specialized care for major diseases, including cancer, heart disease, and mental health, and to train specialists in these fields. This program is certain to attract widespread support because its benefits will be quite apparent throughout the nation, particularly in areas where such specialized treatment has not been readily available in the past. Advances in the field of mental health and new progress in treating the problems of aging are expected to be specially noteworthy.

ENVIRONMENTAL HEALTH. Progress in environmental health activities is likely to be equally marked during the coming decade. This expectation applies particularly to the crucial fields of water supply and water and air pollution control and to the expanded grant program for the construction of waste treatment works and of adequate sewers. It is assumed that public needs in these fields will receive increasing recognition and that this will be reflected in appropriations. Increased resources will also be devoted to studying the health consequences of the use of pesticides and chemical fertilizers. In all these endeavors, cooperation with state and local agencies is expected to continue, with the federal government possibly giving additional financial inducements to state and local authorities. Other areas of increasing expenditures will deal with the problems of waste disposal and the construction of an Environmental Health Center for supervising and centralizing research in the whole field.

Health-Connected Welfare Programs

MATERNAL AND CHILD HEALTH CARE. This field, which has been the responsibility of the Children's Bureau of HEW, will also receive increasing attention. The nation's record of infant mortality is far from enviable, and the rate is higher than in many other advanced countries. Since there is a pronounced correlation between family income levels and infant mortality, increasing stress will be laid on treating this problem on a broader social basis. This will call for higher expenditures, both to keep up with an increasing population and to upgrade the services provided. School health services are another "underdeveloped" segment, and they will receive increasing attention as all medical science makes progress toward stressing preventive medicine and treatment.[3]

MISCELLANEOUS HEALTH SERVICES. These will share in the broad upward trend of expenditures. They comprise a great many activities, ranging from Indian health facilities, and general purpose Public Health Service hospitals, to the compilation of health statistics, to appropriations for retirement pay for commissioned officers of the Public Health Service and the Surgeon General's Office. St. Elizabeths and Freedmen's Hospitals must also be mentioned in this connection.

Labor and Manpower, Including the Unemployment Insurance Trust Fund

While the activities of the Department of Labor include a considerable number of disparate operations, from an expenditure point of view two of these stand out far above all others: expenditures devoted to manpower development and training and the Unemployment Insurance Trust Fund.[4] (See Table 26.)

It must be expected that the Department's major functions will

[3] Model II-B includes expenditures of $900 million annually for a comprehensive school health service for up to 15 million children from disadvantaged families too poor to pay for regular medical attention.

[4] Contributions to the unemployment funds paid on behalf of federal employees are also of some importance here.

become increasingly important. They comprise all matters concerned with labor-management relations, a field that is certain to become more crucial if the hoped-for productivity gains and effective labor-management wage-price guidelines are to be realized. They also include all matters affecting wage and labor standards[5] and the functions of the Bureau of Labor Statistics, the Bureau of International Labor Affairs, and the Secretary's and Solicitor's Offices.

TABLE 26. Model I and Model II: Federal Expenditures on Labor and Manpower, Administrative Budget and Cash Budget, 1963, 1966, 1968, and 1973

(In billions of current dollars for fiscal years)

Item	Actual 1963	Pro-posed 1966	Projected 1968			Projected 1973		
			Model I	Model II-A	Model II-B	Model I	Model II-A	Model II-B
Manpower Administration	0.1	0.5	0.8	0.9	1.1	1.0	1.3	1.8
Others	0.1	0.1	0.1	0.1	0.1	0.2	0.2	0.2
Total, administrative budget	0.3	0.6	0.9	1.0	1.2	1.2	1.5	2.0
Unemployment Insurance Trust Fund[a]	3.8	3.3	3.6	3.5	4.0	6.2	4.7	5.8
Total, cash budget[b]	3.5	3.6	4.2	4.4	5.1	7.4	6.2	7.8
Total, cash budget, as a percentage of GNP	0.6	0.5	0.6	0.6	0.7	0.8	0.6	0.8

Note: Details may not add to totals due to rounding.
[a] This fund combines the expenditures of the federal-state and railroad unemployment systems.
[b] After adjustments for interfund transactions and intergovernmental transfers.

While all these activities are projected to show increased expenditures, they are relatively small compared to the outlays for the Manpower Administration, which are scheduled to account for nearly 90 percent of total expenditures in this classification in the 1966 administrative budget. Nor is this proportion likely to change significantly in the future. Present and future technological developments make for a much more rapid obsolescence of job skills, and it cannot be taken for granted that persons who already have skills may not have to acquire different ones several times during their

[5] Expenditures for federal employees' accident compensation claims are in the functional category of General Government Operations.

working lives. Retraining programs are expected to include about 260,000 adults and youths in 1966. This figure is expected to go up for all our models, as is the expenditure per individual participating in these programs. Model II-B envisages that during the early 1970's about 1 percent of the labor force may be in retraining programs every year if unemployment is not to exceed 4 percent. This would mean providing facilities for about 850,000 persons, and expenditures for this one program may well reach $1.3 billion by 1973.

It is also anticipated that the Manpower Administration will intensify efforts to provide youth employment opportunities, and this will require additional amounts to be provided in the administrative budget as well as in the trust funds. By contrast, appropriations for unemployment benefits to federal employees and ex-servicemen are not expected to rise significantly, higher benefits probably being offset by fewer claimants.

By far the largest disbursements under the jurisdiction of the Department of Labor are from the Unemployment Insurance Trust Fund. These finance the administrative expenses of the former Bureau of Employment Security as well as all federal and state expenditures in connection with the United States Employment Service, in addition to actual benefit payments. (See Table 27.) For 1966, administrative expenses at all levels are scheduled to exceed $500 million. It is expected that in future years substantial improvements can be made in the USES, greatly extending the scope as well as the quality of its services. This will result in increased expenditures, particularly under Model II-B. Projected unemployment compensation payments depend on several contingencies. Most important of these is the rate of economic growth that is assumed and the unemployment rates that are regarded as compatible with such assumptions. In this study we have assumed an unemployment rate of 4 percent for Models II-A and II-B. Model I, based on only present and officially proposed programs, cannot be regarded as consistent with full employment aspirations, particularly over the medium and longer term. Under this assumption a rate of unemployment of over 7 percent would have to be expected by 1973, which would mean sharply increased payments for unemployment benefits. This is reflected in the Model I expenditure figures, which are higher than those under Model II-A in this category.

TABLE 27. Model I and Model II: Rate of Unemployment, Rate of Insured Unemployment, and Benefit Payments, 1963–73

Fiscal year	Net unemployment rate (in percent)		Rate of insured unemployment[a] (in percent)			Benefit payments from Unemployment Insurance Trust Fund[b] (in billions of current dollars)		
	Model I	Models II-A and II-B	Model I	Model II-A	Model II-B	Model I	Model II-A	Model II-B
Actual								
1963[c]		5.7%		4.4%			3.0	
1964		5.0		3.8			2.8	
1965 (prelim.)		4.8		3.7			2.7	
Assumed								
1966		4.5[d]		3.4[d]			2.7[d]	
Projected								
1967	5.4%	4.0	4.3%	3.2	3.5%	3.0	2.7	3.0
1968	5.7	4.0	4.6	3.3	3.6	3.3	2.9	3.4
1969	6.0	4.0	5.0	3.3	3.7	3.8	3.0	3.8
1970	6.3	4.0	5.3	3.4	3.8	4.2	3.2	4.2
1971	6.6	4.0	5.6	3.4	3.9	4.7	3.4	4.6
1972	6.8	4.0	5.9	3.5	3.9	5.1	3.7	4.8
1973	7.1	4.0	6.2	3.5	3.9	5.5	4.0	5.0

[a] Models I and II-A assume the introduction of federal minimum standards of unemployment compensation and a gradual liberalization of the earnings base to $5,600 by 1973. Model II-B assumes further liberalization of standards and benefits.

[b] This fund combines benefit payments under federal-state and railroad unemployment systems.

[c] For 1963 through 1966 identical figures are assumed for all models.

[d] For fiscal 1966, this is the official budget figure.

Another very important assumption concerns the extent of coverage (at present only about 60 percent of the total labor force is covered) and the size of benefits, which currently replace only about 25 percent of all labor income lost because of unemployment. Extensive improvements are projected for all our models; for Model II-B we assume nearly full coverage at a benefit level approximating 60 percent of lost labor income for the overwhelming majority of cases. This would raise the benefit payments to nearly $5 billion by 1973. A possible projection of unemployment benefit payments under these assumptions is shown in Table 27.

Economic Opportunity Programs

The Economic Opportunity Act was passed in 1964 to combat poverty in both urban and rural America. The program authorized under that legislation is included here. (See Table 28.) Some of the component programs are under the direct jurisdiction of the Office of Economic Opportunity (which was created by the Act) in the Executive Office of the President, and some are administered by other agencies, with OEO exercising coordinating jurisdiction. It operates from funds appropriated to the President. The whole program is still in the experimental stage and liable to changes in emphasis and direction. However, the projections reflect our conviction that it will continue to expand during the period under discussion, because the needs are manifest and many of the causes of poverty can be cured only on a long-term basis. The economic opportunity program puts heavy emphasis on youth activities for two reasons. First, unskilled young people are having great difficulty in

TABLE 28. Model I and Model II: Federal Expenditures on Economic Opportunity Programs, Administrative and Cash Budgets, 1966, 1968, and 1973

(In billions of current dollars for fiscal years)

Item	Pro-posed 1966	Projected 1968			Projected 1973		
		Model I	Model II-A	Model II-B	Model I	Model II-A	Model II-B
Community Action	0.5	0.7	0.8	0.9	1.2	1.4	1.8
Job Corps	0.3	0.4	0.6	0.7	0.9	1.1	1.4
Work and training programs	0.5	0.7	0.8	0.9	1.3	1.4	1.8
Other	0.1	0.1	0.2	0.3	0.3	0.4	0.5
Total, administrative and cash budgets	1.3	1.9	2.4	2.8	3.7	4.3	5.5
Total, administrative and cash budgets, as a percentage of GNP	0.2	0.3	0.3	0.4	0.4	0.4	0.5

Note: Details may not add to totals due to rounding.

finding employment. Second, poverty is self-perpetuating from generation to generation, and it is considered best to break this cycle with the generation just entering adult life.

Economic opportunity programs can be classified under four main headings: Community Action programs, the Job Corps, Work and Training programs, and miscellaneous measures. Community Action programs are the largest of these in terms of expenditures. The rationale behind this emphasis is that a successful attack on poverty can best be conducted at the local level by persons and local organizations acquainted with the problems of the poor in their own communities. These programs are designed to provide a framework for coordinating existing policies and programs and to fill any gaps that may be found. Considerable emphasis is laid on small-scale research programs to identify the causes of poverty and on pre-school programs for culturally deprived children. Remedial reading, literacy courses, local leadership courses, and a host of other services are included in these programs, for which the federal government provides 90 percent of all needed funds. We project an increase in the 1966 level of expenditures of slightly under half a billion dollars to about $1.2 billion in 1973 under existing policies (Model I) and over $1.8 billion for Model II-B.

The Job Corps program is among the most important of the youth activities. One part is designed to operate in small rural centers, where young men will be engaged in conservation work, combined with an educational program designed to raise the level of their basic education. Sixteen thousand youths are expected to be enrolled in these rural centers by the end of fiscal 1966. This program is projected to grow very considerably to an annual intake of about 40,000 youths in Model I, rising to over 60,000 in Model II-B. The urban part of the program will provide young men and women with more specialized vocational training as well as an improved general education. At the end of fiscal 1966, 24,000 young people are expected to be enrolled in these urban centers, and our projections foresee a rise similar to that in rural centers, to about 60,000 in Model I and over 100,000 in Model II-B by 1973.

Work and Training programs consist of the Neighborhood Youth Corps, the College Work-Study program, and the Work Experience program. The first two of these are designed for young people. The Neighborhood Youth Corps offers full-time and part-time work to young people 16 to 21 years of age to give them some work experience and added income and thereby prevent them from becoming school dropouts. Those already out of school, in addition to obtaining work experience and incomes, also benefit from remedial education and counseling. It is anticipated that 290,000 youths will be served by the Neighborhood Youth Corps in fiscal 1966, and our projections foresee considerable further growth as the program becomes better established. By 1973 there will be more than 20 million people in the eligible age group.

The College Work-Study program, from which over 100,000 young people are scheduled to benefit in fiscal 1966, is designed to enable academically qualified students from low-income families to remain in college by providing summer and part-time jobs. All of our models provide for considerable increases in the scope of the work-study programs.

In contrast to these measures, whose purpose is to help young people, the Work Experience program is designed for needy, low-income adults to enable them to acquire needed skills and to become self-supporting. It is intended primarily for relief recipients and is used in conjunction with existing state and local programs. In 1966, 112,000 persons are scheduled to be enrolled in this program. The projections assume significant increases in the number aided under the program through 1973, to around 200,000 persons in Model I and to 300,000 in Model II-B. Altogether, work and training programs, estimated to cost slightly under $0.5 billion in 1966, are projected to show growth similar to that of the Community Action programs to about $1.2 billion in Model I and to more than $1.8 billion annually in Model II-B.

Of the important miscellaneous programs in this category, the adult literacy program may well reach a peak of 150,000 persons in a relatively short time. However, it is hoped that before the end of the period under discussion, the need for long-term continuation of this program will have declined because of the provision of a better educational base in schooling for underprivileged children. On the other hand, the VISTA (Volunteers in Service to America) program may well expand considerably from its small base of 5,000 persons in fiscal 1966; this program is designed to develop into a domestic Peace Corps and may well attract many who want to offer their services on a full- or part-time basis with little or no remuneration. Retired persons and housewives are obvious examples, and the tasks that await these volunteers are many and varied.

The granting of "very small" loans to farm families and very small businesses may well expand somewhat in the future. However, this activity will remain one of the less important ones under the Economic Opportunity Act, largely because the individual amounts involved will continue to be small.

It may be asked why we have assumed such significant increases for Economic Opportunity programs if we postulate that the United States is going to be reasonably prosperous. There is no real contradiction here once it is realized that standards of what constitutes poverty are likely to shift upward in line with the general level of incomes. Our projections for Models II-A and II-B also assume an extension of most of these programs to include older people, and II-B assumes that some new programs would be started.

Public Welfare Services

Public welfare services include most of the functions discharged by the Welfare Administration and by the Vocational Rehabilitation Administration of the Department of Health, Education, and Welfare, as well as the school lunch, milk, and food stamp programs of the Department of Agriculture. (See Table 29.)

By far the largest item of expenditures consists of grants to the states for public assistance. This includes programs for old age assistance, medical assistance for the aged, and aid to dependent children, the blind, and the permanently and totally disabled. At present, no federal funds are granted for contributions to the general assistance programs of states and localities.

Under our assumption of reasonably full employment, the public assistance case load would be expected to show first a decrease and later, after the reasonably full employment level has been reached, only small increases in line with population trends. However, welfare expenditures cannot be viewed in isolation. They depend on general economic conditions and also on the content of other social programs (federal, state, and local). Furthermore, rising standards may be reflected in the field of welfare expenditures as in all other segments of the United States economy. This is taken into account, particularly in our assumptions as to the costs of the various service programs, which are projected to rise by a large amount. Conspicuous among these is the new program of medical services for needy children. Expenditures for the Bureau of Family Services, the Office of Aging, and programs to combat juvenile delinquency are also assumed to show substantial increases.

TABLE 29. Model I and Model II: Federal Expenditures for Public Welfare Service, Administrative and Cash Budgets, 1963, 1966, 1968, and 1973

(In billions of current dollars for fiscal years)

Item	Actual 1963	Proposed 1966	Projected 1968			Projected 1973		
			Model I	Model II-A	Model II-B	Model I	Model II-A	Model II-B
Grants to states[a]	2.7	3.5	3.8	4.2	5.0	4.6	5.2	6.8
Vocational rehabilitation administration	0.1	0.2	0.2	0.4	0.5	0.4	0.5	0.7
Department of Agriculture programs[b]	0.3	0.5	0.6	0.7	0.7	0.7	1.2	1.2
Contingencies and new programs					0.2			0.3
Total, administrative and cash budgets	3.1	4.2	4.6	5.3	6.4	5.7	6.9	9.0
Total, administrative and cash budgets, as a percentage of GNP	0.6	0.6	0.6	0.7	0.8	0.6	0.7	0.9

Note: Details may not add to totals due to rounding.
[a] Includes programs for old age assistance, medical assistance for the aged, and aid to dependent children, the blind, and the totally and permanently disabled.
[b] Includes school lunch, milk, and food stamp programs.

The efforts of the Department of Health, Education, and Welfare in the field of vocational rehabilitation are concerned with persons who are suffering from physical and mental disabilities. (General retraining programs are under the jurisdiction of the Department of Labor.) We have projected appreciable increases in the expenditures for the Vocational Rehabilitation Administration because it has been assumed that much more stress will be laid on rehabilitating mentally handicapped persons in future years.

All models show significant increases for the school lunch and special milk programs, due chiefly to increasing school enrollments and the inclusion of more school districts. The food stamp program would be increased to embrace many additional areas, and in Models II-A and II-B it would be nationwide in coverage. Beyond the present programs both Models II-A and II-B envisage that in future years federal contributions for general public assistance payments will be forthcoming and that new programs for providing much better facilities for pre-school and school-age children of working mothers, as well as for pre-school assistance for children from low-income families, will be enacted.

While a number of other plans for general welfare programs have been actively discussed, the authors have not included them in their projections because it was felt that no public consensus on the programs could be expected by 1973, particularly if conditions are generally prosperous. These programs include a comprehensive system of family allowances for children (possibly limited to children after the first or second) or a system of income maintenance payments for the poorest segment of the population. In both cases, costs might be about $15 billion by 1973, or about 1.5 percent of GNP. Family allowances are paid in Canada and have been introduced in most Western European countries. The cost calculation has been based on a rough adaptation of the Canadian scale of benefits, with some increases. Family allowances (which could be subject to income tax) have had their advocates in this country for many years. Their adoption, however, is rendered doubtful by current generally prosperous economic conditions and by the increasing concern felt by many over undue population increases, particularly among low-income families.

On the other hand, a system of income maintenance payments for the poorest segment of the population has found an increasing number of advocates. A variation of this idea is the concept of a "negative income tax" advocated by Professor Milton Friedman of the University of Chicago as a substitute for all other welfare programs. The cost estimate of about $15 billion or slightly more is based on a minimum family income of $3,000 for fiscal 1973, with somewhat more than half this figure for single-person consumer units.[6]

It must be emphasized that not all welfare programs discussed would be additive. For example, the income maintenance proposal

[6] See also James N. Morgan, *et al., Income and Wealth in the United States* (McGraw-Hill, 1962).

would certainly reduce public assistance case loads substantially, and while this would benefit mainly state and local government finances, there would also be significant savings in federal expenditures. Another example is the food stamp program, which could probably be entirely discontinued if an income maintenance plan were adopted, unless it is continued primarily as a farm support measure. These various welfare plans are discussed in some detail because, while we do not believe it likely that they will be in force by 1973, there is a good chance that some of them will be adopted in the later 1970's. Model II-B includes a contingency fund for future programs in this field.

Social Insurance[7]

By far the most important social insurance program is the social security program, which is administered by the Social Security Administration and financed through the Old Age and Survivors Insurance and Disability Insurance trust funds.[8] The civil service retirement and the railroad retirement trust funds are also treated here. (See Table 30.) Since its inception thirty years ago, the social insurance system of the United States has been improved periodically. While our Model I estimates are worked out on the basis of present law and incorporate President Johnson's budget message proposals (including Medicare for the Aged), it would be unrealistic to believe that during the next eight years no further improvements would be built into the system.

Thus Model II-A assumes that social security benefits will rise in line with increases in the cost of living, with an additional annual improvement factor of 1.5 percent, resulting in a total increase in benefits of 3 percent a year. Model II-B makes the further assumption that an annual improvement factor of about 3 percent will be built into the benefit system, resulting in a total increase in benefits of 4.5 percent a year. Similarly, both Models II-A and II-B assume increases in the civil service and railroad retirement pensions and in the payments for Medicare for the Aged.

[7] Unemployment Insurance is included in the section on Labor and Manpower.
[8] The only significant items financed from general revenues are two proposed expenditures; the first would appropriate funds to pay for the liability incurred by the government for military service credits, and the second would finance hospital benefits for aged persons who are not covered by social security.

TABLE 30. Model I and Model II: Federal Expenditures for Social Insurance[a], Administrative and Cash Budgets, 1963, 1966, 1968, and 1973

(In billions of current dollars)

Item	Actual 1963	Proposed 1966	Projected 1968			Projected 1973		
			Model I	Model II-A	Model II-B	Model I	Model II-A	Model II-B
Old-age and survivors, and disability insurance trust funds	15.8	20.4	21.4	22.4	23.1	26.5	32.5	35.7[c]
Medicare for the aged		1.9	2.0	2.1		3.0	3.2	3.4
Civil service and railroad retirement trust funds	2.3	2.8	3.1	3.2	3.5	4.0	4.2	4.4
Transfers from administrative budget								
Health insurance premium subsidies							0.1	2.5
Transfer to OASDI								(2.0)[d]
Total, cash budget[b]	17.8	22.8	26.3	27.5	28.0	33.3	39.5	45.5
Total, cash budget, as a percentage of GNP	3.2	3.5	3.5	3.6	3.7	3.6	3.9	4.5

Note: Details may not add to totals due to rounding.
[a] Excluding unemployment insurance.
[b] After adjustments for interfund transactions and intergovernmental transfers.
[c] Includes transfers of $2 billion from administrative budget.
[d] Included in figure for OASDI.

Model I estimates of OASDI expenditures and of the costs of Medicare for the Aged are based on estimates by Robert J. Myers, Chief Actuary of the Social Security Administration, with some adaptations.[9] Estimates in Models II-A and II-B are based on the same figures and include the improvement factors mentioned above. In the case of Model II-B, the higher improvement factor will cause expenditures to exceed trust fund revenues after 1970. The difference could be met either through increased contributions from employers and employees or in part through a transfer from general revenues (the administrative budget). The latter method is used in most countries of Western Europe. We have assumed that a contribution from general revenues to the extent of $2.0 billion will be

[9] U.S. Social Security Administration, *Actuarial Cost Estimates for the Hospital Insurance Act of 1965 and Social Security Amendments of 1965*, Actuarial Study No. 59 (January 1965).

made for this purpose in fiscal 1973, and this is reflected in administrative budget expenditures for that year.[10] The costs of Medicare for the Aged include only those incurred for social security recipients, at present about 85 to 90 percent of all persons over 65 years of age, with costs for the remainder being met from the general welfare budget; however, with the passage of time nearly the entire population in this age group will be covered through the social security system, and this is reflected in the cost estimates.

Estimates of OASDI expenditures in Models II-A and especially II-B assume that by 1973 "public social security" will form the base for a widespread system of supplementary private pension schemes covering virtually all occupational groups, and that such private benefits will be transferable from job to job as are public benefits. This combination would for the first time constitute a really comprehensive system of caring for the needs of all Americans of retirement age.

Additionally, Model II-B assumes the establishment of a trust fund to help all Americans meet the rapidly growing costs of adequate health care, not indeed by providing universal medical care, but possibly by establishing a system of insurance premium subsidies to enable American families to meet the growing costs of constantly improving standards of adequate health care through private insurance protection. A sum of $2.5 billion is estimated for this purpose in fiscal 1973, to be financed by contributions from the administrative budget. January 1, 1973 is assumed as the starting date for the program. In Model II-A a later effective date is assumed, and only a nominal amount is shown for preparatory expenditures. Should the need for such a development be regarded as not proven, particularly because of the special new programs for the aged and for needy children, it should be borne in mind that private consumer expenditures for medical care increased at an average rate of 8 percent annually during the period 1950-62 and that a continuation of this rate would mean total annual expenditures approaching $55 billion by 1973.

[10] We have not assumed that this "improvement factor" will go so far as to embrace the concept of "dynamic" pensions, which is in force in Germany and under which benefit payments are calculated and revised with reference to recent earnings in the retired individual's former occupation. However, such a plan may well gain acceptance in the future, particularly since somewhat similar provisions are already in force for United States military pensions.

TABLE 31. Model I and Model II: Federal Expenditures for Veterans Benefits and Services, Administrative and Cash Budgets, 1963, 1966, 1968, and 1973

(In billions of current dollars for fiscal years)

Fiscal year	Model I	As a percentage of GNP	Models II-A and II-Bᵃ	As a percentage of GNP
		Administrative Budget		
Actual				
1963	5.2	0.9%		
Proposed				
1966	4.6	0.7		
Projected				
1968	5.7	0.8	6.2	0.8%
1963	6.6	0.7	7.3	0.7
		Cash Budget		
Actual				
1963	6.0	1.1		
Proposed				
1966	5.1	0.7		
Projected				
1968	6.1	0.8	6.7	0.9
1973	7.0	0.8	7.8	0.8

ᵃ Model II-A projections are the same as for Model II-B.

In general, social insurance cost projections assume that such expenditures will be fitted into the pattern of the nation's War on Poverty and that they represent an important weapon in this struggle. Even with the "improvements" assumed in Model II-B, and when combined with welfare and other social programs, as a share of GNP these would still be below the level of current social welfare expenditures in Germany and France. It is anticipated, however, that in the next decade, most Americans will be able to regard these public benefits not as their only source of retirement income but rather as a secure base for additional privately financed benefits.

Veterans Benefits and Services

The principal expenditures in this category (see Table 31) are for service-connected disability compensation, nonservice-connected disability pensions, hospitals and medical care, readjustment benefits, and other benefits and services. There are also various trust funds, the most important one of which is for the veterans life insurance program.

The largest expenditures by far are for compensation for service-connected disability and death, scheduled to run at $4.1 billion in fiscal 1966. In future years the number of compensation cases is likely to fall slightly year by year (see Table 32), but in our projections average benefit payments rise, and for the period under discussion this will more than make up for the declining case load.

By contrast, costs of pensions paid to veterans and their survivors for nonservice-connected death and disability have been rising and will soon exceed those of service-connected compensation. Moreover, this trend is likely to continue. As of 1965, World War I veterans and their dependents constituted about 70 percent of the case load, but payments to veterans of World War II and the Korean conflict and their survivors must be expected to rise as increasing numbers of veterans reach ages at which the rates of disability and mortality mount.

We have assumed in Model I a continuation of the veterans compensation and pension programs provided for in existing legislation, but Models II-A and II-B include the cost of a number of

TABLE 32. Projected Veteran Population in Civilian Life and Number Receiving Compensation and Pension Payments, 1963, 1968, and 1973

(Fiscal years)

Item	Actual 1963	Projected 1968	Projected 1973
Veterans in civilian life[a] (in millions)	22.0	21.1	20.0
Under 55 years of age	18.4	16.7	13.6
55–64	1.3	2.3	4.3
Over 64	2.3	2.1	2.1
Compensation claims[b] (in thousands)			
Disability cases	1,987	1,996	1,996
Death cases	375	360	349
Pension claims[b] (in thousands)			
Disability cases	1,182	1,240	1,200
Death cases	779	1,045	1,250

Source: Estimates based on figures supplied by the Veterans Administration, October 1964, as revised.
[a] On June 30 of each year.
[b] Average number of cases during fiscal year.

proposed increases.[11] The total cost would amount to nearly $800 million annually in fiscal 1967, gradually declining to a rate of over $600 million by fiscal 1973, as the number of World War I veterans declines. With the general improvement of old age benefits we assumed that the pressure for special veterans' benefits will diminish.

Hospital and Medical Care

At over $1.2 billion, expenses for hospital and medical care are large and must be expected to increase further under the double impact of increasing medical and hospital costs and the higher age distribution of the veteran population. It should also not be forgotten that the quality of services provided to veterans has been continually improved. Hospital construction costs will be a continuing item, particularly because of modernization requirements and population shifts.

Readjustment Benefits

Expenditures for veterans' education are expected to decline in Model I. Under existing law, they will concern only orphans of war veterans because the program for Korean War veterans has expired. The sale of certificates of participation in the direct housing loans and housing loan guarantees for veterans have given these programs net receipts in recent years. This is expected to continue, though on a declining scale, because the portfolio of desirable loans is shrinking. In addition, veterans' benefits under this program are running out gradually. Extension of all G.I. bill benefits (education, insurance, housing) to all post-Korean servicemen has been suggested. We assumed that some new veterans' legislation might be adopted before 1973 and therefore have included a contingency allowance in Models II-A and II-B.

Personnel and Administrative Expenses

The Veterans Administration has an outstanding record of achieving greater productivity in its operation, undoubtedly helped by automation. This trend is expected to continue, and we have as-

---

[11] We have not included the American Legion proposal for a general pension of $100 monthly for all World War I veterans.

sumed a gradual decline in the number of personnel, except in the medical care category.

Trust fund expenditures are confined almost exclusively to payments under the veterans' life insurance program. We have projected that these will remain in the range of $450 million to $650 million, depending partly on the choice of dates for insurance dividend disbursements.

Agriculture

Practically all programs in this functional category are the responsibility of the Department of Agriculture. The only significant exception is the Farm Credit Administration, which is a public enterprise. Its activities are important only in connection with trust fund expenditures and affect the consolidated cash budget.

The Department of Agriculture's far-flung activities reach into almost every county across the nation. Most of its responsibilities are included in this functional category, with the exception of the Food for Peace program already discussed under International Affairs and Finance (in Chapter VII); the milk, school lunch, and food stamp programs, which fall under the Public Welfare Services category above; and the Forest Service, which is treated under Natural Resources (in Chapter VIII). Because the Department carries on many varied activities, in any projection of its future role, each of its major components must be examined if the aggregate figures are to be meaningful.[12]

For the program component that includes the Agricultural Stabilization and Conservation Service and the Soil Conservation Service, we have assumed a slowly rising trend of expenditures throughout the period under review for all models. We feel that whatever changes take place in agricultural price support policy, farm income will continue to be supported by a variety of devices, and that these programs will figure prominently among them. This does not imply that exactly the same measures will be used in the future. However, such programs as watershed and flood protection, conservation operations, and some aspects of the Soil Bank will not disappear without similar ones replacing them. Further, it is likely

---

[12] These are the Agricultural Stabilization and Soil Conservation Service, the Commodity Credit Corporation, and the Farmers Home Administration.

in the case of program changes that the shift in expenditures will be toward these items. While for the Department as a whole some net reduction in expenditures has been assumed, this does not rule out substantial shifts among the various types of expenditures. In the budget's functional classification, expenditures for farm income stabilization, including those for price support programs, make up 70 percent of all expenditures for agriculture and agricultural resources. This implies that there may be considerable flexibility in the choice of methods to achieve this objective.

Commodity Credit Corporation operations, which account for about 50 percent of all departmental expenditures today, are projected to run at lower levels than in the early 1960's, with a gradual decline to 1973. For Models II-A and II-B we have assumed a radical change to a greater emphasis on income payments on a per farm basis, accompanied by a drastic reduction in price supports. These would be retained only to put a low floor under prices (possibly at 50 percent of a revised parity formula), and this implies reliance on the free market for nearly all sales of agricultural commodities. However, since Congress will probably not agree to a drastic cut in farm incomes for smaller farmers, income payments will continue to be sizable. Of course a new office might be set up to administer such payments, but it seems best to discuss them in this context, since they would be designed to replace most Commodity Credit Corporation expenditures.

Another major component consists of the Rural Electrification Administration and Farmers Home Administration. Concerning the latter, it is anticipated that the direct loan program will be replaced by a proposed loan insurance program for rural housing, resulting in considerable budgetary "savings." As to the Rural Electrification Administration, in Models II-A and II-B it is assumed that the practice of making loans at 2 percent interest will be replaced entirely either by financing through the private market or at the very least on terms not more favorable than the interest costs on such loans to the government. All models assume acceptance of the President's proposals that the REA be given authority to operate a revolving fund. This would result in an equal decrease in budget expenditures and receipts.

In contrast to these major programs, the host of functions performed by the Department of Agriculture in a variety of smaller programs will continue to expand. They include the Extension, Foreign Agricultural, Agricultural Marketing, Agricultural Research, Economic Research, Statistical Reporting, and the Rural Community Development Services and a number of general administrative and statistical activities. The scope of these activities is likely to increase in the future, and account has been taken of this in the projections, as shown in Table 33.

TABLE 33. Model I and Model II: Federal Expenditures for Agriculture, Administrative and Cash Budgets, 1963, 1966, 1968, and 1973

(In billions of current dollars for fiscal years)

Fiscal year	Administrative Budget			Consolidated Cash Budget^a					
	Model I	Model II-A	Model II-B	Model I	As a percentage of GNP	Model II-A	As a percentage of GNP	Model II-B	As a percentage of GNP
Actual 1963	5.2			5.7	1.0%				
Proposed 1966	3.9			4.1	0.6				
Projected 1968	4.8	4.4	4.2	5.0	0.7	4.6	0.6%	4.3	0.6%
1973	4.8	4.4	4.1	5.0	0.5	4.6	0.5	4.1	0.4

^a Includes the Farm Credit Administration.

Housing and Community Development

Housing and Home Finance Agency

Projections for the Housing and Home Finance Agency are full of pitfalls, mainly because this agency is made up in part of a number of quasi-independent units[13] and also because for many programs receipts from premiums and other charges and the sale of assets provide all or most of the financing. (See Table 34.) A direct charge on the federal budget is not involved. The greatest difficulties in making estimates and projections are caused by fluctuations in the amounts realized from the sale of assets, mortgages and direct loans, and real estate holdings since these depend on the

[13] The Public Housing Administration, the Federal Housing Administration, and the Federal National Mortgage Association.

TABLE 34. Model I and Model II: Federal Expenditures for Housing and Community Development, Administrative and Cash Budgets[a], 1963, 1966, 1968, and 1973

(In billions of current dollars for fiscal years)

Item	Actual 1963	Pro- posed 1966	Projected 1968			Projected 1973		
			Model I	Model II-A	Model II-B	Model I	Model II-A	Model II-B
Urban mass transportation	very small	small	0.2	0.3	0.5	0.4	0.6	1.1
Urban Renewal Administration[b]	0.2	0.4	0.6	0.8	0.9	1.2	1.5	2.1
Federal Housing Administration	0.1	−0.1	−0.2	−0.2	−0.2	−0.3	−0.3	−0.3
Federal National Mortgage Association	−0.4	−0.5	−0.2	−0.2	−0.2	in balance		
Public Housing Administration	0.2	0.2	0.3	0.4	0.5	0.5	0.7	1.1
Other Housing and Home Finance Agency and contingency fund	small	0.1	0.3	0.7	0.8	0.4	0.9	2.0
Federal Home Loan Bank Board[c]	−0.3	−0.3	−0.3	−0.4	−0.4	−0.4	−0.5	−0.5
District of Columbia	0.1	0.1	0.1	0.1	0.2	0.1	0.1	0.2
Total, administrative budget	−0.1	in balance	0.8	1.5	2.1	1.9	3.0	5.7
Trust funds and adjustments	−0.2	0.7	0.8	0.8	0.9	0.9	1.0	1.2
Total, cash budget	−0.3	0.7	1.6	2.3	3.0	2.8	4.0	6.9
Total, cash budget, as a percentage of GNP	—	0.1	0.2	0.3	0.4	0.3	0.4	0.7

Note: Details may not add to totals due to rounding.
[a] Minus figures indicate an excess of sales of assets from portfolios and other receipts over expenditures.
[b] Includes urban mass transportation proposed expenditure of $48 million for 1966.
[c] Includes Federal Savings and Loan Insurance Corporation.

state of the money market and on a number of other factors. Therefore, the over-all budget figures of the agency do not measure the total activity generated by the financial outlays of its many branches. As for the future, the need for greatly expanded urban renewal and development programs is plain, though there is some difference of opinion as to whether the present institutional setting should be changed. While it is expected that promoting the agency to the status of a full-fledged department would meet some of the organizational problems, it must be emphasized that the needs for better housing and community development require more comprehensive programs, irrespective of any institutional changes. However, in this field most programs take a long time to be fully effective, and for this reason actual expenditures can be increased only gradually.

Despite these limitations, practically all of the various programs of the Housing and Home Finance Agency are projected as showing substantial increases. One of the most striking increases is scheduled to occur in urban mass transportation, an expenditure currently made by the Office of the Administrator. The federal government provides assistance through loans, grants, or demonstration projects for existing planned local mass transit systems. In Model I expenditures are estimated to reach $400 million by 1973, with $1 billion projected for Model II-B. Indeed, the main limiting factor for such expenditures is the long lead-time necessary for planning and developing mass rapid transit systems.

Among the activities under the direct control of the Administrator of HHFA, those carried out by the Urban Renewal Administration require by far the largest outlays. Its largest expenditures are incurred in providing federal assistance, amounting to 66⅔ percent (in some cases 75 percent) of net costs, to local governments for the acquisition, redevelopment, and rehabilitation of slums and blighted areas.

The major portion of expenditures for urban renewal are being incurred in connection with the write-down of land acquisition costs to bring these costs to a level low enough to stimulate private development. However, other grant programs, such as those for relocating families and businesses, for urban planning, and for open-space land, are also important. Furthermore new, imaginative programs may well supplement those currently in operation during the course of the coming decade. At present there is a serious lag, often lasting more than five years, between the approval of an urban renewal project and the time when significant expenditures are actually made. Our projections reduce this time lag appreciably, but it is a limiting factor in forecasts of Urban Renewal Administration expenditures. The resources devoted to this field will depend on the priority that the nation assigns to the rebuilding and rehabilitation of its urban areas. Our models assume increasing expenditures, reaching $1.2 billion in Model I and $2 billion in Model II-B by 1973.

Of the HHFA expenditures grouped under the Community Facilities Administration, public facility loans and advances for public works planning may have less scope for expansion. The same may apply to the Housing for the Elderly program if, as is intended, more of its financing comes from federally guaranteed loans from private sources. There is considerable potential for expansion of planning, research, and demonstration activities in this field, which, although they have a limited budgetary impact in themselves, are likely to spawn new programs that could become significant in the future.[14]

Public Housing Administration

The Public Housing Administration's main responsibility since its inception has been the administration of the low-rent public housing program. Its most important expenditures by far have been its annual contributions to local authorities to reduce the cost of public housing. Currently well over 500,000 units are assisted by these annual payments. While the need for low-income housing is likely to persist, the general public housing program has come under increasing criticism, and this has been reflected in our estimate of only 50,000 new units to be constructed annually under Model I. A significant number of these would be special units for the elderly, for which there is considerable community support. Such a program would necessitate total annual subsidies exceeding $500 million. Model II-B assumes a doubling of the rate of construction to 100,000 units by 1973, which would raise total expenditures to $600-$700 million annually. In addition, a new program of "spot" rehabilitation of existing private housing, suitable particularly for larger families, has just been undertaken. In the future this may well involve rent subsidies for private accommodations for large families, because their needs are often not met by public

[14] College Housing Loans are treated under Assistance to Higher Education in Chap. VIII.

housing. The program's potential is very great and, if successful, it could well require expenditures of $200-$400 million annually by fiscal 1973. This is reflected in our Models II-A and II-B. In time the image of public housing would change considerably under the impact of the new programs.

Federal Housing Administration

The Federal Housing Administration is responsible principally for the programs of government-insured mortgages for homes and apartment buildings. It is also responsible for issuing loans for home modernization and repair and for various specially assisted mortgage programs. Its activities fluctuate in line with economic conditions, the availability of private credit on favorable terms, and a number of other factors. In most years, and despite an irregularly rising trend of mortgage defaults during the last decade, premium and other income has been more than enough to meet the agency's responsibilities in loan defaults and other expenses. Its excess of receipts over expenditures has served to reduce the total net budgetary resources devoted to the housing field. Our projections assume a continuation of this trend, though we realize that if such surpluses become too large, there will undoubtedly be considerable pressure to reduce insurance premiums for mortgage programs insured by the Federal Housing Administration. The suggested program of federally insured private loans to finance the acquisition and development of land for new towns and communities might fall within the responsibility of the FHA.

Federal National Mortgage Association

The Federal National Mortgage Association's main function is to provide a market for federally insured mortgages for special programs. It has been outstandingly successful in discharging its functions. It is particularly valuable to private builders at times of general credit stringency. In addition, imaginative use can be made of its facilities to promote socially desirable housing programs for which private financing would not be readily forthcoming. Examples are the provision of mortgages bearing below-market interest rates for housing for families with low or moderate incomes, and a new proposed program for mortgage insurance for land development which would be too speculative for most conventional private lenders.

FNMA holds a large stock of mortgages, acquired mostly in times of over-all credit stringency. In recent years proceeds from the sales of such assets have considerably exceeded all of the Association's expenditures, resulting in a surplus which was available to reduce other budgetary outlays in the housing field. It is difficult to project the future of this program, and we have assumed that the Association's operations after 1968 will have a generally neutral effect on the federal budget.

Federal Savings and Loan Insurance Corporation

By contrast, it is estimated that the Federal Savings and Loan Insurance Corporation, which insures savings institutions, will have moderately increasing annual surpluses if generally prosperous conditions continue, since premiums should continue to exceed claims by a comfortable margin each year. These surpluses will continue to be available to reduce net budgetary expenditures in this field.

Contingency Fund

Model II-B contains an estimate for a contingency fund. Since housing and community development is an area where urgent unsatisfied needs will continue to exist and where new ideas and programs could gain acceptance in the next few years, additional expenditure estimates are included for such programs.

District of Columbia

Estimates of future federal payments to the District of Columbia to help defray expenses of the District government and for its services to the federal government show a slow but steady upward trend. In Models II-A and II-B an additional annual contribution toward the expenses of constructing and operating a subway system has been assumed.

Trust Funds

Finally, projections have been made for trust funds in this classification. The secondary market operations of the revolving fund of the FNMA fluctuate considerably from year to year. We have projected purchases to exceed sales somewhat in most years, thus imposing a net charge of $100-$200 million annually on the cash budget. The main reason for this is that we expect moderately increasing building activity over the period. For the same reason, the Federal Home Loan Bank Board would require additional capital funds from time to time. District of Columbia municipal government trust fund projections reflect judgments as to the likely level of tax rates and public services in the District during the decade, as well as estimates of population and requirements.

CHAPTER X

General Government

THE GENERAL GOVERNMENT classification comprises many major and minor agencies. Included here are the judiciary, most of the legislative branch,[1] the Executive Office, most of the Treasury Department (except the Coast Guard and interest on the debt), the General Services Administration, most of the Department of Justice, the Civil Service Commission, and some functions of other departments[2] and many minor agencies. (See Table 35.) Expenditures for interest payments on the federal debt are treated separately in this chapter.

The Judiciary, the Legislative Branch, and the Executive Office of the President

While this is one of the small sectors of public expenditures, outlays in these areas have risen steadily in the recent past, and this trend is expected to continue in the interest of good and efficient government. Increases in population and incomes and the growing

[1] The Library of Congress is included under Education and Research in Chap. VIII.

[2] Central personnel management functions of the Department of Labor and expenditures for territories and possessions, including the Ryukyu Islands and the Panama Canal Zone.

complexity of modern life will render inevitable increased expenditures for "the central nervous system" of our government operations.

The cost of the judiciary is assumed to go up by over 50 percent during the period under discussion. Larger increases are projected for the legislative branch, because to make legislative processes more efficient major increases in professional staffs are required, particularly for congressional committees.

TABLE 35. Model I and Model II: Federal Expenditures for General Government[a], Administrative and Cash Budgets, 1963, 1966, 1968, and 1973

(In billions of current dollars for fiscal years)

Item	Actual 1963	Proposed 1966	Projected 1968		Projected 1973	
			Model I	Models II-A and II-B	Model I	Models II-A and II-B
Legislative, Judiciary, Executive Office	0.2	0.3	0.3	0.4	0.4	0.6
Treasury Department	0.7	0.8	1.0	1.1	1.2	1.4
Justice Department	0.3	0.4	0.4	0.5	0.6	0.8
General Services Administration	0.5	0.6	0.7	0.8	0.9	1.1
Miscellaneous general government functions	0.3	0.3	0.3	0.3	0.4	0.4
	—	—	—	—	—	—
Total, administrative budget	2.1	2.4	2.7	3.1	3.5	4.3
Trust funds	—	—	—	—	—	—
Total, cash budget	2.0	2.4	2.7	3.1	3.5	4.3
Total, cash budget, as a percentage of GNP	0.4	0.3	0.4	0.4	0.4	0.4

Note: Details may not add to totals due to rounding.
[a] All figures are net after adjustments.

Expenditures for the Executive Office of the President[3] are projected as increasing in about the same proportion as those of the legislative branch, but the dollar amounts involved are relatively small. Models II-A and II-B also anticipate a growth in the functions and importance of the Bureau of the Budget and the Council

---

[3] Excludes the Office of Economic Opportunity, which, although part of the Executive Office, is classified under Welfare.

of Economic Advisers because of the increasing importance of economic factors in the affairs of the nation.

Treasury Department

The Internal Revenue Service is by far the largest of the Treasury Department's operations and accounts for the lion's share of all noninterest expenditures of the Department, exclusive of the Coast Guard. We have projected a rise in IRS expenditures in line with increasing numbers of taxpayers and more effective tax enforcement.

Other Treasury operations comprise the Offices of the Secretary and the Treasurer, the Bureaus of Accounts, Public Debt, Customs, the Mint, Engraving and Printing, and Narcotics, as well as the United States Secret Service. All of these perform essential and continuing functions of the federal government. We have not assumed any organizational changes, though it might be desirable to transfer the Bureau of Narcotics to the Department of Health, Education, and Welfare for humanitarian reasons. Expenditures are highest for the Bureau of Customs. With the envisaged increases in world trade and the explosive rise in world travel, even lower tariffs would not offset an increase in its activities. It is assumed that expenses of the Bureaus of Accounts and the Public Debt, as well as of most other Treasury operations, will rise about in line with general government operations. The United States Mint and the Secret Service are projected as having above-average increases, the former because of the growing demand for coins and the possible substitution of base-metal for silver coinage, as well as the impending modernization of its outdated facilities. Expenditures for the Secret Service will increase to expand the protective capabilities of the Service.

In Models II-A and II-B, expenditures are projected at a somewhat higher level in line with the generally increased activities of the federal government.

Department of Justice

The operations of the Department of Justice include legal activities and general administration, the Federal Bureau of Investigation, the Federal Prison System, and the Immigration and Naturalization Service. Expenditures in the first category are assumed to increase about in line with general government operations, but those for the Immigration and Naturalization Service lag behind increases in other operations because no unusual gain in immigration is assumed. By contrast, expenditures of the FBI are projected to rise more than proportionately because the scope of its activities in combating serious crime and its involvement in civil rights enforcement will increase at the expense of local police departments with their limited jurisdictions. Provision for expenditures for a general system of public defenders or equivalent representation in federal cases is included in the estimates.

For Models II-A and II-B a number of new programs are envisaged: a program of federal grants for better training facilities for local police forces and a program of matching grants to help the states improve their prison facilities. Expenditure estimates for these models also include payments to victims of crimes of violence in federal cases. This would be similar to the system recently introduced in England.

General Services Administration

The General Services Administration performs a most important "housekeeping" function for the whole federal establishment. It is concerned with all aspects of the construction, maintenance, and operation of public buildings. Expenditures for these purposes are projected to show substantial increases, particularly in Models II-A and II-B, as the government is expected to construct more buildings for its own occupancy rather than rely on rented space.

On the other hand, activities other than those connected with real property are expected to show less-than-average increases, particularly because continuing gains in the efficiency of inventory management are anticipated, and these could go far to neutralize the pressure generated by the increasing activities of the federal government.

Miscellaneous General Government Functions

These include the various territorial government responsibilities of the Department of the Interior (Guam, Pacific Trust Territories,

Virgin Islands) and the Department of Defense (Panama Canal Zone and Ryukyu Islands). The Bureau of Employees' Compensation in the Department of Labor handles accident compensation and medical payments for federal government employees and is also included in this section. Other agencies that fall within this category include the Civil Service Commission, the General Accounting Office, and a number of minor ones. Expenditures for these miscellaneous functions are expected to increase moderately in line with total federal expenditures.

Interest on the Federal Debt

Illustrative projections of interest costs have to be deferred until all other income and expenditure items have been estimated. Only then can one of the prime determinants of the interest cost—the size of the federal debt—be ascertained. The other main determinant, of course, is the anticipated level of interest rates.

Interest rate projections are obviously affected substantially by our assumptions about taxes. In Chapter V we have worked out revenue estimates on the basis of existing tax rates, incorporating only those changes recommended in the President's 1966 budget. We have pointed out, however, that the surpluses resulting under these assumptions may not permit the attainment of the assumed rate of economic growth. This applies to Model I to only a small extent, and therefore for this model interest charges have been computed assuming no future change in tax rates. It applies more definitely to Model II-A, for which considerably reduced taxes and/or a method of revenue sharing with state and local governments would be imperative if the assumed growth objectives are to be reached. However, we have not estimated the exact time and size of future tax reductions because they depend on the development of all the factors in the private sector of the economy.

This poses a problem for our calculation of interest costs, particularly for the years after fiscal 1968, when "surpluses" under Model II-A assumptions would pile up, assuming unchanged tax rates and steady economic growth.

Therefore, for the purpose of calculating interest costs for Models II-A1 and II-A2, we have arbitrarily assumed that in practice large budget surpluses would not be allowed to develop and have calculated interest costs on the assumption of a balanced cash budget. It is immaterial in this context whether this balance is achieved through tax reduction or by other means.

Calculations are complicated by several other factors: one concerns the interest-bearing composition of the existing debt structure and whether existing obligations originated in times when lower or higher interest rates prevailed. Another factor concerns assumptions about the prevailing maturity dates of the debt. For many years critics of debt-management policy have contended that the maturities of the existing federal debt are much too short, making debt management unduly difficult because of the lack of freedom to manipulate maturity dates. A debt stretch-out, or long-term funding of the debt, is regarded as eminently desirable by the critics. One obstacle has been the rigid 4.25 percent interest limitation on United States Government debt issues of more than five years' maturity. Thus, in addition to assumptions about the likely trend of interest rates, interest cost projections must make an assumption about the probability of repeal of this interest limitation. If this should be indicated, a further assumption must be made about the extent to which the new freedom may in fact be used. Another complication will stem from the surpluses in certain trust funds that will accrue increasingly after fiscal 1965. The interest payments to federal trust funds from investments in United States Government securities appear in the administrative budget, but not in the figures for the consolidated cash budget because payments to the public are not involved. Federal expenditures for interest are shown in Table 36.

We have taken year-by-year administrative budget surpluses and deficits as determinants of the size of the debt on which interest must be paid. For the cash budget we have subtracted from these the added interest cost occasioned by surpluses in the social security trust funds. We have also assumed a slight gradual hardening of interest rates, but no really tight money policy.

The somewhat higher interest cost of financing the federal debt is due partly to the fact that many bonds, originally issued in earlier years when interest rates were lower, will reach their maturity dates and must be replaced by higher-yielding bonds. In part, it is due also to our assumption of a gently rising level of interest rates in a period of reasonably full employment. We do not assume that more than minor progress will be made in lengthening the maturity dates

TABLE 36. Model I and Model II: Federal Expenditures for Interest (Department of the Treasury), Administrative and Cash Budgets, 1963, 1966, 1968, and 1973

(In billions of current dollars for fiscal years)

Fiscal year	Model I	As a percentage of GNP	Model II-AI	As a percentage of GNP	Model II-A2	As a percentage of GNP	Model II-B	As a percentage of GNP
Administrative Budget								
Actual								
1963	10.0	1.8%						
Proposed								
1966	11.6	1.7						
Projected								
1968	12.5	1.7	12.8	1.7%	12.5	1.6%	13.1	1.7%
1973	12.5	a	13.3b	1.3	13.3b	1.3	13.5	1.3
Consolidated Cash Budget								
Actual								
1963	7.4	1.3						
Proposed								
1966	8.8	1.3						
Projected								
1968	9.6	1.3	9.6	c	9.5	1.2	9.8	1.3
1973	10.0	1.1	10.5b	1.0	10.5b	1.1	10.7	1.1

[a] The percentage is 1.35.
[b] On the basis of the illustrative "surpluses" arising under the assumption of no tax reduction, the interest on the federal debt would be about $1.5–$2.0 billion lower.
[c] The percentage is 1.25.

of the debt structure, even if the 4.25 percent interest limitation is repealed, because it is felt that cost considerations will bar any ambitious refunding that would undoubtedly be necessary to accomplish such an objective.

Concluding Remarks

The program-by-program discussion in the preceding four chapters may suggest to the reader a confidence of the authors in their own prescience which they do not pretend to have. A budget projection can show "what is in the cards," but how the cards will be played is another question. Our emphasis has been on budget projections in the perspective of economic growth. Some readers may feel that our estimates of future budget expenditures are very high, but they may be surprised to find that the ratio of projected federal expenditures to a conservatively estimated increase in GNP remains approximately constant.

The growing GNP will result in rising taxable incomes, profits, and payrolls, which will make it possible to finance additional or growing expenditure programs without increases in tax rates. In turn, the expanding expenditure programs will support the increase in consumer expenditures and open opportunities for rising business investment. Here we are not only counting on the so-called multiplier effect of government expenditures but also on what has been called the leverage effect. Programs in our age that require government participation, for example: urban development; rapid air and surface transportation; and atomic, space, oceanic, and other research and development programs, can create a need for large-scale private productive investments.

We have presented various alternative projections. One is based on present legislation and policies, including the proposals in President Johnson's program. Another group of projections assumes that over the years new programs or program expansions now in the discussion stage will be adopted. Particularly for the later parts of the period covered, projections would be wholly unrealistic if they did not assume that some programs will move from the discussion to the adoption stage while other programs may be reduced. Because of the uncertainty, we have presented this model in two variations, one with higher, the other with lower allowances for new or expanding programs. The projection with the lower estimates would give room for and would necessitate another substantial reduction in revenues by tax cut or sharing of tax revenues with state and local governments. In the case of the alternative with a more substantial increase in expenditures, further tax reductions would be of only limited size.

The presentation of alternatives makes it clear that the projections are meant to be neither unconditional forecasts nor recommendations of future policy. They are presented as tools to be used by those who consider and appraise future federal budgets and fiscal policy. It was our specific aim to test the feasibility of projecting federal budgets for a number of years. We believe our experience in preparing these projections demonstrates the desirability and feasibility of viewing the budget for the ensuing year in the light of longer-term revenue and expenditure developments and in recognition of the fact that government budgets are influenced by, and in turn influence, economic growth. We are aware that presenting official projections by the government may at times appear politically inexpedient. Projections prepared and published by private, nonpolitical research organizations may help to overcome political hesitations.

Appendix Tables

All figures and projections in the following tables are presented on the basis of the income and product accounts of the Department of Commerce before the revisions published in August 1965 and subsequent months.

The over-all difference in levels of GNP is of the order of about 1 percent. Significant for our study is the upward revision of the figures for business profits. This revision has some effect on our projections for corporate profits tax receipts. Thus, the revenue projections may be slightly understated in the study; the difference, however, is not likely to be very substantial.

The changes in the two sets of estimates are not likely to have any significant effect on the expenditure side of our projections. The upward revision of GNP will result in a very slightly lower percentage of total GNP being devoted to federal expenditures in all our models. The difference may amount to 0.2 percent. Consequently budget surpluses would be slightly higher and appear at a somewhat earlier date than projected, thus giving added weight to our conclusion that in the absence of greatly increased defense expenditures, some combination of further tax cuts and additional financial support for state and local governments will be necessary for the achievement of the assumed rates of growth in all our models.

Figures for fiscal 1963 are the actual receipts and expenditures for that year. Figures for fiscal 1966 are from the 1966 budget document. Those for later years are projections made by the authors, except for Table A-1, which is from the National Economic Projection Series of the National Planning Association and is given here for purposes of comparison.

Figures in parentheses in the following tables are estimates that are unrealistic in the absence of additional measures. For an explanation, see Chapter I, Table 2, p. 9.

TABLE A-1. Nation's Economic Budgets, Selected Years, 1960–74[a]

(In billions of current dollars)

Calendar Year	Item	Disposable receipts	Purchases of goods and services	Excess of receipts	Disposable receipts as a percentage of GNP	Purchases of goods and services as a percentage of GNP
	Households	349.9	328.2	21.6	69.6%	65.3%
	Domestic investment	50.7	71.8	−21.1	10.1	14.3
	Net international	1.6	3.0	− 1.4	0.3	0.6
	Government	103.5	99.6	3.9	20.6	19.8
1960	Federal[b]	56.6	53.1	3.5	11.3	10.6
	State and local	46.9	46.5	0.4	9.3	9.2
	Statistical discrepancy	−3.0	—	− 3.0	−0.6	—
	Gross National Product	502.6	502.6	—	100.0	100.0
	Households	402.6	373.2	29.4	68.8	63.8
	Domestic investment	60.6	82.3	−21.7	10.4	14.1
	Net international	1.7	4.4	− 2.7	0.3	0.8
1963	Government	123.4	125.1	− 1.7	21.1	21.4
	Federal[b]	63.5	66.3	− 2.8	10.8	11.4
	State and local	59.9	58.8	1.1	10.3	10.0
	Statistical discrepancy	−3.3	—	− 3.3	−0.6	—
	Gross National Product	585.0	585.0	—	100.0	100.0
	Households	547.2	502.9	44.3	66.9	61.5
	Domestic investment	93.8	127.6	−33.8	11.5	15.6
	Net international	0.9	9.0	− 8.1	0.1	1.1
1969	Government	175.9	178.3	− 2.4	21.5	21.8
	Federal[b]	77.7	77.7	—	9.5	9.5
	State and local	98.2	100.6	− 2.4	12.0	12.3
	Gross National Product	817.8	817.8	—	100.0	100.0
	Households	727.1	668.2	58.9	66.4	61.0
	Domestic investment	131.3	177.4	−46.1	12.0	16.2
	Net international	1.0	8.5	− 7.5	0.1	0.8
1974	Government	235.6	240.9	− 5.3	21.5	22.0
	Federal[b]	87.6	87.6	—	8.0	8.0
	State and local	148.0	153.3	− 5.3	13.5	14.0
	Gross National Product	1,095.0	1,095.0	—	100.0	100.0

Source: *National Economic Projections to 1974* (National Planning Association, Center for Economic Projections, 1964).

[a] This table provides a general frame for economic projections. The estimates of federal receipts and purchases are not strictly comparable with those presented in the text and tables of this book.

[b] Federal grants-in-aid are deducted from federal revenues and shown as state and local receipts in order to prevent double counting.

TABLE A-2. Model I: Selected Projections of the United States Economy, Fiscal Years 1963, 1968, and 1973[a]

Item (In millions)	Actual 1963	Projected 1968	Projected 1973
Population	188.5	203.0	220.0
Total labor force	75.2	81.0	87.3
Civilian labor force	72.4	78.5	85.0
Unemployment as a percentage of the civilian labor force	5.7	5.7	7.1

(In billions of current or constant dollars)	Actual 1963 Current	Projected 1968 Current	Projected 1968 Constant	Projected 1973 Current	Projected 1973 Constant
Gross National Product	568.0	739.5	688.5	921.5	804.8
Personal income	452.1	586;5	546.1	740.0	646.3
Disposable personal income	392.7	511.5	476.3	636.5	557.7
Personal consumption expenditures	365.9	473.0	440.4	591.0	516.1
Corporate profits	48.6	67.5	62.8	73.5	64.2
Gross private domestic investment	79.5	104.5	97.3	145.0	126.6
Total government receipts	162.9	(205.0)	(190.8)	(273.0)	(238.4)
Total government expenditures	163.9	211.5	196.9	273.0	238.4
Total government purchases of goods and services	119.2	154.0	143.3	206.0	179.9
Federal government receipts[b]	109.6	(136.0)	(126.7)	(174.0)	(152.0)
Federal government expenditures[b]	112.3	142.5	132.7	167.0	145.9
Federal government purchases of goods and services	63.6	70.5	65.6	77.5	67.7

[a] Assuming a 3.1 percent annual growth rate in real terms; also assumed is a 1.3 percent annual price increase for the current dollar figures. Constant dollar figures based on fiscal year 1963 prices.

[b] Federal government revenue and expenditure projections in accordance with national income accounts figures. Figures in parentheses are estimates that are unrealistic in the absence of additional measures. See Chap. I, Table 2, p. 9.

TABLE A-3. Models II-A and II-B: Selected Projections of the United States Economy, Fiscal Years 1963, 1968, and 1973[a]

Item (in millions)	Actual 1963	Projected 1968 Model II-A	Projected 1968 Model II-B	Projected 1973 Model II-A	Projected 1973 Model II-B
Population	188.5	203.0		220.0	
Total labor force	75.2	81.4		89.4	
Civilian labor force	72.4	79.0	79.2	87.0	87.5
Unemployment as a percentage of the civilian labor force	5.7%	4.0%		4.0%	

(In billions of current or constant dollars)	Actual 1963 Current	Projected 1968 Current Model II-A1	Current Model II-A2	Current Model II-B	Projected 1968 Constant Model II-A1	Constant Model II-A2	Constant Model II-B	Projected 1973 Current Model II-A1	Current Model II-A2	Current Model II-B	Projected 1973 Constant Model II-A1	Constant Model II-A2	Constant Model II-B
Gross national product	568.0	771.0	771.0	771.0	715.2	715.2	715.2	1,007.5	1,007.5	1,007.5	867.8	867.8	867.8
Personal income	452.1	604.5	604.5	604.5	560.8	560.8	560.8	786.0	786.0	786.0	677.0	677.0	677.0
Disposable personal income	392.7	528.0	528.0	528.0	489.8	489.8	489.8	682.0	682.0	682.0	587.4	587.4	587.4
Personal consumption expenditures	365.9	490.5	490.5	490.5	455.0	455.0	455.0	634.0	634.0	634.0	546.0	546.0	546.0
Corporate profits	48.6	76.1	76.1	76.1	70.6	70.6	70.6	99.5	99.5	99.5	85.7	85.7	85.7
Gross private domestic investment	79.5	112.5	112.5	112.5	104.4	104.4	104.4	165.0	165.0	165.0	142.1	142.1	142.1
Total government receipts	162.9	(216.0)	(216.0)	216.0	(200.4)	(200.4)	200.4	(290.0)	(290.0)	291.5	(249.8)	(249.8)	251.1
Total government expenditures	163.9	229.0	226.0	230.0	212.4	209.6	213.4	286.0	269.0	293.5	246.3	231.7	252.8
Total government purchases of goods and services	119.2	158.0	155.0	159.0	146.6	143.8	147.5	212.0	203.5	208.3	182.6	175.3	179.4
Federal government receipts[b]	109.6	(144.5)	(144.5)	144.5	(134.0)	(134.0)	134.0	(197.0)	(197.0)	198.5	(169.7)	(169.7)	171.0
Federal government expenditures	112.3	147.0	144.0	152.0	136.4	133.6	141.0	181.0	172.5	197.0	155.9	148.6	169.7
Federal government purchases of goods and services	63.6	72.5	69.5	73.2	67.3	64.5	67.9	79.0	70.5	76.0	68.0	60.7	65.5

Source: See Table A-2.

[a] Assuming the attainment of "reasonably full employment" during fiscal 1967 and a 4 percent annual growth rate in real terms thereafter. Also assumed is a 1.5 percent annual price increase for the current dollar figures. Constant dollar figures are based on fiscal 1963 prices.

[b] Federal government receipts and expenditures projections in accordance with national income accounts figures. Figures in parentheses are estimates that are unrealistic in the absence of additional measures. See Chap. I, Table 2, p. 9.

TABLE A-4. Model I: Average Number of All Federal Government Employees, Fiscal Years, 1963, 1968, and 1973[a]

Agency	Actual 1963	Projected 1968	Projected 1973
Legislative Branch	24,500	26,200	28,400
Judiciary	5,890	6,200	6,600
Executive Office	1,849	1,700	2,000
Foreign Economic Assistance	14,400	16,900	17,400
Department of Agriculture	87,681	86,900	85,900
Department of Commerce	28,967	52,900	65,100
Department of Defense—Military	1,020,000	900,000	800,000
Department of Defense—Civil	46,655	48,100	48,100
Office of Economic Opportunity		9,000	21,800
Department of Health, Education, and Welfare	79,350	103,300	119,000
Department of the Interior	63,960	78,000	88,800
Department of Justice	32,436	34,900	37,100
Department of Labor	8,442	11,200	15,800
Department of State	23,291	26,000	27,800
Post Office Department	581,112	624,300	658,700
Treasury Department	116,177	125,400	130,000
Atomic Energy Commission	6,984	7,600	8,000
Federal Aviation Agency	45,014	50,500	58,000
General Services Administration	33,101	41,500	47,400
Housing and Home Finance Agency	13,559	17,600	23,700
National Aeronautics and Space Administration	26,044	37,000	34,000
Veterans Administration	172,000	167,000	157,000
National Science Foundation	875	1,400	1,800
U. S. Information Agency	11,629	12,500	12,900
Small Business Administration	3,222	3,500	3,700
Other independent agencies (including Export-Import Bank)	34,785	37,600	40,000
Tennessee Valley Authority	17,292	17,800	18,000
Total[b]	2,499,215	2,545,000	2,557,000

[a] Our figures include employment in the legislative and judicial branches of the federal government. Differences between our "average number of all employees" projections and the Budget Bureau's end-of-June employment estimates are as follows:

    1. NPA projections for the Treasury Department include military personnel for the Coast Guard (about 30,000 each year).

    2. NPA projections for the Commerce Department include temporary employees for the Census Bureau in census years.

    3. NPA projections for the Agriculture Department do not include seasonal employees, who are included in the end-of-June Budget Bureau estimates (about 35,000 each year.)

    4. Rapidly growing agencies, such as NASA, show fewer employees on the average computation basis than on the Budget Bureau's end-of-June basis.

[b] Details may not add to totals due to rounding.

TABLE A-5. Model I: Federal Government Receipts, by Source (in Current Dollars), Cash Budget and Administrative Budget, 1963–73

(In billions of current dollars)

Fiscal year	GNP	Personal income	Corporate profits[a]	Total receipts, cash budget[a]	As a percentage of GNP	Total receipts, administrative budget[a]	As a percentage of GNP
Actual							
1963	568.0	452.1	48.6	109.7	19.3%	86.4	15.2%
1964	604.0	477.5	54.7	115.5	19.1	89.5	14.8
Proposed							
1965	640.0	508.5	61.2	117.4	18.4	91.2	14.2
1966	681.5	538.5	66.0	123.5	18.1	94.4	13.9
Projected[b]							
1967	(709.5)	(560.0)	(66.7)	(131.0)	(18.5)	(97.2)	(13.7)
1968	(739.5)	(586.5)	(67.5)	(137.9)	(18.6)	(100.9)	(13.6)
1969	(773.0)	(614.5)	(68.5)	(146.7)	(18.9)	(105.2)	(13.6)
1970	(807.5)	(643.5)	(69.6)	(152.8)	(18.9)	(109.8)	(13.6)
1971	(844.0)	(673.5)	(71.0)	(159.9)	(18.9)	(114.7)	(13.6)
1972	(882.0)	(705.0)	(72.3)	(167.4)	(19.0)	(119.9)	(13.6)
1973	(921.5)	(737.0)	(73.5)	(175.2)	(19.0)	(125.3)	(13.6)

[a] After adjustments and rounding.
[b] Figures in parentheses are estimates that are unrealistic in the absence of additional measures. See Chap. I, Table 2, p. 9.

TABLE A-6. Model I: Federal Government Receipts, by Source (in Constant Dollars), Cash Budget and Administrative Budget, Selected Years, 1963–73

(In billions of constant fiscal 1963 dollars)

Fiscal year	GNP	Personal income	Corporate profits	Total receipts, cash budget[a]	Total receipts, administrative budget[a]
Actual					
1963	568.0	452.1	49.4	109.7	86.4
Proposed					
1966	651.5	514.8	63.1	118.1	90.1
Projected					
1968[b]	(688.5)	(546.1)	(62.8)	(128.4)	(93.9)
1973	(804.8)	(646.3)	(64.2)	(153.0)	(109.4)

[a] After adjustments and rounding.
[b] Figures in parentheses are estimates that are unrealistic in the absence of additional measures. See Chap. I, Table 2, p. 9.

TABLE A-7. Model I: Federal Government Receipts by Source, Administrative Budget, 1963–73[a]

(In billions of current dollars)

Fiscal year	Individual income tax	Corporation income tax	Excise tax[b]	Estate and gift taxes	Customs	Miscella- neous[c]	Total[d]
Actual							
1963	47.6	21.6	9.9	2.2	1.2	3.9	86.4
1964	48.7	23.5	10.2	2.4	1.3	3.4	89.5
Proposed							
1965	47.0	25.6	10.7	2.8	1.4	3.7	91.2
1966	48.2	27.6	9.8	3.2	1.5	4.1	94.4
Projected							
1967[e]	(50.3)	(28.2)	(10.2)	(3.3)	(1.6)	(3.6)	(97.2)
1968	(52.7)	(28.9)	(10.5)	(3.4)	(1.7)	(3.7)	(100.9)
1969	(55.5)	(29.6)	(11.0)	(3.5)	(1.8)	(3.8)	(105.2)
1970	(58.5)	(30.3)	(11.6)	(3.6)	(1.9)	(3.9)	(109.8)
1971	(61.8)	(30.9)	(12.3)	(3.7)	(2.0)	(4.0)	(114.7)
1972	(65.3)	(31.5)	(13.1)	(3.8)	(2.1)	(4.1)	(119.9)
1973	(69.0)	(32.0)	(14.0)	(3.9)	(2.2)	(4.2)	(125.3)

[a] Assuming no tax cut except for the excise tax cut proposed in the fiscal 1966 budget.
[b] Excise taxes less automotive-related taxes that go into the highway trust fund.
[c] Less interfund transactions.
[d] Details may not add to totals due to rounding.
[e] Figures in parentheses are estimates that are unrealistic in the absence of additional measures. See Chap I, Table 2, p. 9.

TABLE A-8. Model I: Receipts of Federal Trust Funds, by Source, 1963–73

(In billions of current dollars)

Fiscal year	Employment taxes[a]	Unemployment tax deposits by states	Veterans' life insurance premiums	Highway trust fund	Miscellaneous trust receipts	Federal employees' retirement fund	Interest on trust funds	Total trust fund receipts	Inter-government transactions[b]
Actual									
1963	14.9	3.0	0.5	3.3	2.7	1.9	1.5	27.7	−4.3
1964	16.8	3.0	0.5	3.5	2.8	2.0	1.6	30.3	−4.3
Proposed									
1965	16.7	3.0	0.5	3.6	2.8	2.2	1.7	30.5	−4.3
1966	18.7	2.9	0.5	4.0	3.5	2.2	1.9	33.7	−4.5
Projected									
1967[c]	(22.7)	(3.0)	(0.5)	(4.2)	(3.7)	(2.3)	(2.0)	(38.4)	(−4.6)
1968	(25.3)	(3.2)	(0.5)	(4.4)	(3.8)	(2.4)	(2.1)	(41.7)	(−4.7)
1969	(28.5)	(3.5)	(0.5)	(4.6)	(3.9)	(2.5)	(2.2)	(45.7)	(−4.8)
1970	(29.8)	(3.8)	(0.5)	(4.8)	(4.0)	(2.6)	(2.4)	(47.9)	(−4.9)
1971	(31.1)	(4.2)	(0.5)	(5.0)	(4.1)	(2.7)	(2.6)	(50.2)	(−5.0)
1972	(32.4)	(4.6)	(0.5)	(5.2)	(4.2)	(2.8)	(2.8)	(52.5)	(−5.0)
1973	(33.8)	(5.0)	(0.5)	(5.4)	(4.3)	(2.9)	(3.0)	(54.9)	(−5.0)

[a] Assuming that the administration proposals for social security, Medicare for the aged, and unemployment taxes will be enacted.
[b] To arrive at figures for the consolidated cash budget, interfund transactions must be deducted when adding administrative budget and trust fund receipts.
[c] Figures in parentheses are estimates that are unrealistic in the absence of additional measures. See Chap. I, Table 2. p. 9.

166

TABLE A-9. Models II-A and II-B: Federal Government Receipts, by Source (in Current Dollars), Cash Budget and Administrative Budget, 1963–73[a]

(In billions of current dollars)

Fiscal year	GNP	Personal income	Corporate profits	Total receipts, cash budget		As a percentage of GNP		Total receipts, administrative budget	As a percentage of GNP
				Model II-A	Model II-B	Model II-A	Model II-B		
Actual									
1963	568.0	452.5	49.4	109.8	109.8	19.3%	19.3%	86.3	15.2%
1964	604.0	477.5	54.7	115.5	115.5	19.1	19.1	89.5	14.8
Proposed									
1965	640.0	507.0	61.2	117.4	117.4	18.3	18.3	91.2	14.3
1966	681.5	538.5	66.0	123.5	123.5	18.1	18.1	94.4	13.9
Projected									
1967[b]	(725.3)	(571.5)	(71.0)	(135.6)	135.6	(18.7)	18.7	(101.3)	(14.0)
1968	(771.0)	(604.5)	(76.0)	(146.4)	146.4	(19.0)	19.0	(108.7)	(14.1)
1969	(813.3)	(636.5)	(80.3)	(157.2)	157.2	(19.3)	19.3	(115.4)	(14.2)
1970	(858.0)	(670.0)	(84.8)	(166.6)	167.8	(19.4)	19.6	(122.5)	(14.3)
1971	(905.2)	(706.0)	(89.4)	(176.7)	177.9	(19.5)	19.7	(130.0)	(14.4)
1972	(955.0)	(745.0)	(93.9)	(187.3)	188.6	(19.6)	19.7	(137.9)	(14.4)
1973	(1,007.5)	(786.0)	(99.5)	(198.4)	199.7	(19.7)	19.8	(146.2)	(14.5)

[a] All figures after adjustments and rounding.
[b] Figures in parentheses are estimates that are unrealistic for Model II-A in the absence of additional measures. See Chap. I, Table 2, p. 9.

TABLE A-10. Models II-A and II-B: Federal Government Receipts, by Source (in Constant Dollars), Cash Budget and Administrative Budget, Selected Years, 1963–73[a]

(In billions of constant fiscal 1963 dollars)

Fiscal year	GNP	Personal income	Corporate profits	Total receipts, cash budget		Total receipts, administrative budget
				Model II-A	Model II-B	
1963	568.0	452.1	48.6	109.8	109.8	86.3
1966	651.5	514.8	63.1	118.1	118.1	90.2
1968[b]	(715.2)	(560.8)	(70.6)	(135.8)	135.8	(100.8)
1973	(867.8)	(677.0)	(85.7)	(170.9)	172.0	(125.9)

[a] All figures after adjustments and rounding.
[b] Figures in parentheses are estimates that are unrealistic for Model II-A in the absence of additional measures. See Chap. I, Table 2, p. 9.

TABLE A-11. Models II-A and II-B: Federal Government Receipts, by Source, Administrative Budget, 1963–73[a]

(In billions of current dollars)

Fiscal year	Individual income tax	Corporation income tax	Excise tax[b]	Estate and gift taxes	Customs	Miscella- neous[c]	Total[d]
Actual							
1963	47.6	21.6	9.9	2.2	1.2	3.9	86.4
1964	48.7	23.5	10.2	2.4	1.3	3.4	89.5
Proposed							
1965	47.0	25.6	10.7	2.8	1.4	3.7	91.2
1966	48.2	27.6	9.8	3.2	1.5	4.1	94.4
Projected							
1967[e]	(52.2)	(29.8)	(10.5)	(3.6)	(1.6)	(3.6)	(101.3)
1968	(56.0)	(31.9)	(11.3)	(4.0)	(1.8)	(3.7)	(108.7)
1969	(59.7)	(33.4)	(12.2)	(4.4)	(1.9)	(3.8)	(115.4)
1970	(63.5)	(35.2)	(13.0)	(4.8)	(2.0)	(4.0)	(122.5)
1971	(67.5)	(37.0)	(13.9)	(5.2)	(2.2)	(4.2)	(130.0)
1972	(71.7)	(38.9)	(14.9)	(5.6)	(2.4)	(4.4)	(137.9)
1973	(76.2)	(40.9)	(16.0)	(6.0)	(2.6)	(4.5)	(146.2)

[a] Assuming no tax cut except for the excise tax cut proposed in the fiscal 1966 budget.
[b] Excise taxes less automotive-related taxes that go into the highway trust fund.
[c] Less interfund transactions.
[d] Details may not add to totals due to rounding.
[e] Figures in parentheses are estimates that are unrealistic for Model II-A in the absence of additional measures. See Chap. I, Table 2, p. 9.

TABLE A-12. Models II-A and II-B: Receipts of Federal Trust Funds, by Source, 1963–73

(In billions of current dollars)

Fiscal year	Employment taxes[a] Model II-A	Employment taxes[a] Model II-B	Unemployment tax deposits by states	Veterans' life insurance premiums	Highway trust fund Model II-A	Highway trust fund Model II-B	Miscellaneous trust fund receipts	Federal employees' retirement	Interest on trust funds	Total trust fund receipts Model II-A	Total trust fund receipts Model II-B	Intergovernment transactions[b]
Actual												
1963	14.9	14.9	3.0	0.5	3.3	3.3	2.7	1.9	1.5	27.7	27.7	−4.3
1964	16.8	16.8	3.0	0.5	3.5	3.5	2.8	2.0	1.6	30.3	30.3	−4.3
Proposed												
1965	16.7	16.7	3.0	0.5	3.6	3.6	2.8	2.2	1.7	30.5	30.5	−4.3
1966	18.7	18.7	2.9	0.5	4.0	4.0	3.5	2.2	1.9	33.7	33.7	−4.5
Projected												
1967[c]	(23.2)	23.2	(2.8)	(0.5)	(4.2)	4.2	(3.7)	(2.3)	(2.1)	(38.9)	38.9	(−4.6)
1968	(26.0)	26.0	(3.0)	(0.5)	(4.4)	4.4	(3.8)	(2.4)	(2.3)	(42.4)	42.4	(−4.7)
1969	(29.4)	29.4	(3.2)	(0.5)	(4.6)	4.6	(3.9)	(2.5)	(2.5)	(46.6)	46.6	(−4.8)
1970	(31.1)	31.2	(3.4)	(0.5)	(4.8)	5.8	(4.0)	(2.6)	(2.7)	(49.1)	50.2	(−4.9)
1971	(32.9)	33.1	(3.6)	(0.5)	(5.0)	6.0	(4.1)	(2.7)	(2.9)	(51.7)	52.9	(−5.0)
1972	(34.8)	35.0	(3.8)	(0.5)	(5.2)	6.2	(4.2)	(2.8)	(3.2)	(54.5)	55.7	(−5.0)
1973	(36.7)	36.9	(4.0)	(0.5)	(5.4)	6.5	(4.3)	(2.9)	(3.4)	(57.2)	58.5	(−5.0)

[a] Including administration proposals contained in the 1966 budget.
[b] To arrive at figures for the consolidated cash budget, interfund transactions must be deducted when adding administrative budget and trust fund receipts.
[c] Figures in parentheses are estimates that are unrealistic for Model II-A in the absence of additional measures. See Chap. I, Table 2, p. 9.

169

TABLE A-13. Models I and II: Federal Government Receipts (in Constant Dollars), by Source, National Income Accounts, Selected Fiscal Years, 1963–73[a]

(In billions of constant fiscal 1963 dollars)

Item	Actual 1963	Proposed 1966	Projected 1968	Projected 1973
MODEL I[c]				
Personal taxes[b]	50.1	49.9	(53.1)	(64.6)
Corporate profits tax accruals	22.1	23.6	(26.3)	(27.5)
Indirect business taxes[b]	15.2	15.4	(16.1)	(20.0)
Contributions for social insurance	22.1	26.8	(31.2)	(39.8)
Total[d]	109.6	115.7	(126.7)	(152.0)
MODEL II-A[c]				
Personal taxes[b]	50.1	49.9	(56.6)	(71.7)
Corporate profits tax accruals	22.1	23.6	(18.8)	(35.2)
Indirect business taxes[b]	15.2	15.4	(17.2)	(22.0)
Contributions for social insurance	22.1	26.8	(31.5)	(40.7)
Total[d]	109.6	115.7	(134.0)	(169.7)
MODEL II-B				
Personal taxes[b]	50.1	49.9	56.6	71.7
Corporate profits tax accruals	22.1	23.6	28.7	35.2
Indirect business taxes[b]	15.2	15.4	17.2	23.0
Contributions for social insurance	22.1	26.8	31.5	41.1
Total[d]	109.6	115.7	134.0	171.0

[a] Assumes no change in law other than administration proposals.
[b] Includes some receipts from sources other than taxes.
[c] Figures in parentheses are estimates that are unrealistic in the absence of additional measures. See Chap. I, Table 2, p. 9.
[d] Details may not add to totals due to rounding.

TABLE A-14. Model I: Federal Government Expenditures by Function, Cash Budget, 1963–73

(In billions of current dollars for fiscal years)

Item	Actual		Proposed					Projected			
	1963	1964	1965	1966	1967	1968	1969	1970	1971	1972	1973
Defense-related											
Department of Defense	50.6	51.5	49.9	49.9	50.0	50.0	50.0	50.0	50.0	50.0	50.0
Atomic Energy Commission	2.8	2.8	2.7	2.5	2.6	2.7	2.8	2.9	3.0	3.1	3.2
Other		0.2	0.2	0.1	0.1	0.1	0.1	0.1	0.1	0.1	0.1
Subtotal	53.4	54.5	52.8	52.5	52.7	52.8	52.9	53.0	53.1	53.2	53.3
Nondefense											
International	3.8	3.5	3.6	4.2	4.4	4.8	5.0	5.2	5.3	5.4	5.5
Space research and technology	2.6	4.2	4.9	5.1	5.5	6.0	6.0	6.0	6.0	6.0	6.0
Agriculture	5.7	5.8	4.6	4.1	4.7	5.0	5.0	5.0	5.0	5.0	5.0
Natural resources	2.5	2.6	2.8	2.9	3.1	3.3	3.4	3.5	3.6	3.7	3.9
Commerce and transportation	5.8	6.5	7.4	6.5	7.5	8.1	8.6	9.1	9.5	9.9	10.4
Housing and community development	-0.3	1.7	-0.2	0.7	1.2	1.6	1.8	2.0	2.2	2.5	2.8
Health	1.3	1.7	1.8	2.2	2.5	2.8	3.1	3.5	3.9	4.3	4.7
Labor and manpower[a]	3.5	3.6	3.5	3.6	3.8	4.2	4.8	5.4	6.0	6.6	7.4
Economic opportunity program		—	0.3	1.3	1.6	1.9	2.2	2.5	2.9	3.3	3.7
Public welfare services	3.1	3.5	3.6	4.2	4.4	4.6	4.8	5.0	5.2	5.4	5.7
Social insurance[a]	17.8	18.6	19.7	22.8	24.5	26.0	27.5	29.0	30.5	31.9	33.3
Education and research[b]	1.2	1.3	1.5	2.6	3.5	4.3	5.1	6.0	6.5	7.3	8.0
Veterans' benefits and services	6.0	6.1	6.0	5.1	5.6	6.1	6.4	6.6	6.8	6.9	7.0
General government	2.0	2.2	2.4	2.4	2.5	2.7	2.8	3.0	3.1	3.3	3.5
Interest	7.4	8.0	8.5	8.8	9.2	9.6	9.9	10.1	10.2	10.2	10.0
Total, defense-related and nondefense	115.8	123.8	123.2	129.0	136.7	143.8	149.3	154.9	159.8	164.9	170.2
Adjustments	-2.0	-3.4	-1.8	-1.6	-2.0	-2.0	-2.1	-2.2	-2.3	-2.5	-2.5
Total after adjustments	113.8	120.3	121.4	127.4	134.7	141.8	147.2	152.7	157.5	162.4	167.7
Total expenditures as a percentage of GNP	20.0	19.9	19.0	18.7	19.0	19.2	19.0	18.9	18.7	18.4	18.2

a Unemployment insurance is included in Labor.
b Research expenditures in this category include only the National Science Foundation and new research programs.

TABLE A-15. Models II-A1 and II-A2: Federal Government Expenditures by Function, Cash Budget, 1967–73

(In billions of current dollars for fiscal years)

Item	1967 Model II-A1	1967 Model II-A2	1968 Model II-A1	1968 Model II-A2	1969 Model II-A1	1969 Model II-A2	1970 Model II-A1	1970 Model II-A2	1971 Model II-A1	1971 Model II-A2	1972 Model II-A1	1972 Model II-A2	1973 Model II-A1	1973 Model II-A2
							Projected							
Defense-related														
Department of Defense	50.0	48.5	50.0	47.0	50.0	46.0	50.0	44.5	50.0	43.0	50.0	41.5	50.0	40.5
Atomic Energy Commission	2.6	2.6	2.7	2.6	2.8	2.7	2.9	2.8	3.0	2.8	3.1	2.9	3.2	3.0
Other	0.1	0.1	0.1	0.1	0.1	0.1	0.1	0.1	0.1	0.1	0.1	0.1	0.1	—
Subtotal	52.7	51.2	52.8	49.7	52.9	48.8	53.0	47.4	53.1	45.9	53.2	44.5	53.3	43.5
Nondefense														
International	4.8		5.5		6.0		6.6		7.2		7.8		8.5	
Space research and technology	4.5		4.0		4.0		4.0		4.0		4.0		4.0	
Agriculture	4.4		4.6		4.6		4.6		4.6		4.6		4.6	
Natural resources	3.2		3.6		3.7		3.8		4.0		4.2		4.4	
Commerce and transportation	7.6		8.7		9.2		9.8		10.3		10.9		11.5	
Housing and community development	1.5		2.3		2.6		3.0		3.3		3.6		4.0	
Health research and services	2.7		3.2		3.6		4.0		4.5		5.0		5.5	
Labor and manpower[a]	4.0		4.4		4.7		5.0		5.3		5.7		6.2	
Economic opportunity program	1.8		2.4		2.8		3.2		3.6		4.0		4.3	
Public welfare services	4.7		5.3		5.5		5.8		6.2		6.5		6.9	
Social insurance	25.5		27.5		29.5		32.0		34.5		37.0		39.5	
Education and research[b]	3.6		4.8		5.6		6.6		7.6		8.6		9.5	
Veterans' benefits and services	6.0		6.7		7.0		7.2		7.4		7.6		7.8	
General government	2.7		3.1		3.3		3.5		3.7		4.0		4.3	
Interest	9.2		9.6	9.5	9.7	9.6	9.9	9.8	10.1		10.4		10.5	
Total, defense-related and nondefense	138.9	137.4	148.5	145.3	154.7	150.5	162.0	156.3	169.4	162.2	177.1	168.4	184.8	175.0
Adjustments	−2.0	−2.0	−2.0	−2.0	−2.1	−2.1	−2.2	−2.2	−2.3	−2.3	−2.4	−2.4	−2.5	−2.5
Total after adjustments	136.9	135.4	146.5	143.3	152.6	148.4	159.8	154.1	167.1	159.9	174.7	166.0	182.3	172.5
Total expenditures as a percentage of GNP	18.9	18.7	19.0	18.6	18.8	18.2	18.6	18.0	18.5	17.7	18.3	17.4	18.1	17.1

[a] Unemployment insurance is included in Labor.
[b] Research expenditures in this category include only the National Science Foundation and new research programs.

TABLE A-16. Model II-B: Federal Government Expenditures by Function, Cash Budget, 1967–73

(In billions of current dollars for fiscal years)

Item	1967	1968	Projected 1969	1970	1971	1972	1973
Defense-related							
Department of Defense	48.5	47.0	46.0	44.5	43.0	41.5	40.5
Atomic Energy Commission	2.6	2.6	2.7	2.8	2.8	2.9	3.0
Other	0.1	0.1	0.1	0.1	0.1	0.1	—
Subtotal	51.2	49.7	48.8	47.4	45.9	44.5	43.5
Nondefense							
International	5.5	7.0	8.0	8.8	9.5	10.5	11.8
Space research and technology	6.0	7.0	8.0	8.5	8.0	7.5	6.5
Agriculture	4.2	4.3	4.3	4.3	4.2	4.2	4.1
Natural resources	3.4	3.9	4.1	4.3	4.5	4.7	5.0
Commerce and transportation	7.8	9.2	10.0	10.6	11.3	12.1	12.9
Housing and community development	2.0	3.0	3.6	4.2	5.0	6.0	6.9
Health research and services	2.8	3.7	4.3	5.0	5.7	6.4	7.2
Labor and manpower[a]	4.3	5.1	6.0	6.5	7.0	7.5	7.8
Economic opportunity program	2.0	2.8	3.5	4.0	4.5	5.0	5.5
Public welfare	5.2	6.4	6.8	7.3	7.8	8.4	9.0
Social insurance[a]	25.7	28.0	30.7	33.5	36.5	39.7	45.5
Education and research[b]	3.7	5.3	6.5	8.0	9.5	11.0	12.5
Veterans' benefits and services	6.0	6.7	7.0	7.2	7.4	7.6	7.8
General government	2.7	3.1	3.3	3.5	3.7	4.0	4.3
Interest	9.2	9.8	10.0	10.3	10.6	10.7	10.7
Total, defense-related and nondefense	141.7	155.0	164.9	173.4	181.1	189.8	201.0
Adjustments	−2.0	−2.0	−2.1	−2.2	−2.3	−2.4	−2.5
Total, after adjustments	139.7	153.0	162.8	171.2	178.8	187.4	198.5
Total expenditures as a percentage of GNP	19.2	19.8	20.0	20.0	19.8	19.6	19.7

[a] Unemployment insurance is included in Labor.
[b] Research expenditures in this category include the National Science Foundation and new research programs.

TABLE A-17. Models I and II: Federal Government Expenditures by Function, Cash Budget, Selected Fiscal Years, 1963–73

(In billions of constant fiscal 1963 dollars)[a]

Item	Actual 1963	Proposed 1966	1968 Model I	1968 Model II-A1	1968 Model II-A2	1968 Model II-B	1973 Model I	1973 Model II-A1	1973 Model II-A2	1973 Model II-B
National Security, International, and Space										
Defense-related activities[b]	53.4	50.2	49.2	49.0	46.1	46.1	46.6	45.9	37.5	37.5
International affairs and finance	3.8	4.0	4.5	5.1	5.1	6.5	4.8	7.3	7.3	10.2
Space research and technology	2.6	4.9	5.6	3.7	3.7	6.5	5.2	3.4	3.4	5.6
Total	59.8	59.1	59.2	57.8	54.9	59.1	56.6	56.7	48.2	53.2
Economic Development										
Natural resources	2.5	2.8	3.1	3.3	3.3	3.6	3.4	3.8	3.8	4.3
Commerce and transportation	5.8	6.2	7.5	8.1	8.1	8.5	9.1	9.9	9.9	11.1
Education and research[c]	1.2	2.5	4.0	4.5	4.5	4.9	7.0	8.2	8.2	10.8
Total	9.5	11.5	14.6	15.9	15.9	17.1	19.5	21.9	21.9	26.2
Welfare Expenditures										
Agriculture	5.7	3.9	4.7	4.3	4.3	4.0	4.4	4.0	4.0	3.5

Housing and community development	−0.3	0.7	1.5	2.1	2.1	2.8	2.4	3.4	3.4	5.9
Health services and research	1.3	2.1	2.6	2.9	2.9	3.4	4.1	4.7	4.7	6.2
Labor and manpower[d]	3.5	3.4	3.9	4.1	4.1	4.7	6.5	5.3	5.3	6.7
Economic opportunity program	—	1.2	1.8	2.2	2.2	2.6	3.2	3.7	3.7	4.7
Public welfare services	3.1	4.0	4.3	4.9	4.9	5.9	5.0	5.9	5.9	7.8
Social insurance[d]	17.8	21.8	24.2	25.5	25.5	26.0	29.1	34.0	34.0	39.2
Veterans' benefits and services	6.0	4.9	5.7	6.2	6.2	6.2	6.1	6.7	6.7	6.7
Total	37.1	42.1	48.6	52.3	52.3	55.7	60.8	67.9	67.9	80.8
General Government Operations										
General government	2.0	2.3	2.5	2.9	2.9	2.9	3.0	3.7	3.7	3.7
Interest	7.4	8.4	8.9	8.9	8.8	9.1	8.8	9.0	9.0	9.2
Total	9.4	10.7	11.5	11.8	11.7	12.0	11.8	12.7	12.7	12.9
Total expenditures, cash budget	115.8	123.3	133.9	137.8	134.8	143.8	148.8	159.2	150.7	173.1
Adjustments	−2.0	−1.5	−1.9	−1.9	−1.9	−1.9	−2.2	−2.2	−2.2	−2.2
Total after adjustments[e]	113.8	121.8	132.0	135.9	132.9	141.9	146.6	157.0	148.6	171.0
Total expenditures as a percentage of GNP	20.0	18.7	19.2	19.0	18.6	19.8	18.2	18.1	17.1	19.7

175

a For current dollar table, see Chap. VI, pp. 78-79.
b Includes the Department of Defense and the Atomic Energy Commission.
c Research expenditures in this category include only the National Science Foundation and new research programs.
d Unemployment insurance is included in Labor.
e Details may not add to totals due to rounding.

TABLE A-18. Models I and II: Federal Government Expenditures by Agency, Administrative Budget, Selected Years, 1963–73

(In billions of current dollars for fiscal years)

Agency	Actual 1963	Proposed 1966	Projected 1968 Model I	Model II-A1	Model II-A2	Model II-B	Projected 1973 Model I	Model II-A1	Model II-A2	Model II-B
Legislative Branch	0.1	0.2	0.2	0.3		0.3	0.3	0.4		0.4
Judiciary and Executive Office	0.1	0.1	0.1	0.1		0.1	0.1	0.2		0.2
Funds appropriated to the President	0.3	0.3	0.3	0.2		0.2	0.3	0.3		0.5
Foreign Economic Assistance	2.0	2.2	2.5	2.6		3.2	2.6	4.0		5.5
Department of Agriculture	7.7	6.4	6.0	7.0		6.5	7.0	6.9		6.7
Department of Commerce	0.7	0.8	1.4	1.6		1.8	2.0	2.3		2.6
Department of Defense—Military[a]	50.0	49.0	49.0	49.0	46.5	46.5	49.0	49.0	40.0	40.0
Department of Defense—Civil	1.1	1.3	1.3	1.4		1.5	1.5	1.7		1.9
Department of Health, Education, and Welfare	4.9	7.8	10.6	11.6		13.5	16.6	19.9		28.7
Office of Economic Opportunity	—	1.3	1.9	2.4		2.8	3.7	4.3		5.5
Department of the Interior	1.0	1.2	1.6	1.7		1.9	1.8	2.2		2.5
Department of Justice	0.3	0.4	0.4	0.5		0.5	0.6	0.8		0.8
Department of Labor	0.3	0.6	0.9	1.0		1.2	1.2	1.5		2.0
Post Office Department	0.8	0.7	0.7	0.7		0.7	1.0	1.0		0.5
Department of State[b]	0.4	0.4	0.5	0.7		1.3	0.6	1.7		3.1
Treasury Department	1.1	1.4	1.5	1.7		1.8	1.8	2.2		2.3
Interest	10.0	11.6	12.5	12.8	12.5	13.1	12.5	13.3	13.3	13.5

Atomic Energy Commission	2.8	2.5	2.7	2.7	2.6	2.6	3.4	3.4	3.0	3.0
Federal Aviation Agency	0.7	0.8	1.2	1.4		1.6	1.5	1.9		2.2
General Services Administration	0.5	0.6	0.7	0.8		0.8	0.9	1.1		1.1
Housing and Home Finance Agency	0.4	0.5	1.1	1.8		2.3	2.2	3.4		6.0
National Aeronautics and Space Administration	2.6	5.1	6.0	4.0		7.0	6.0	4.0		6.5
Veterans Administration	5.2	4.6	5.7	6.2		6.2	6.6	7.3		7.3
National Science Foundation[c]	0.2	0.4	0.6	0.8		0.9	0.9	1.2		1.8
U. S. Information Agency	0.2	0.2	0.2	0.3		0.4	0.4	0.4		0.6
Small Business Administration	0.1	−0.2	0.1	0.2		0.3	0.1	0.4		0.5
Federal Home Loan Bank Board	−0.3	−0.3	−0.4	−0.4		−0.4	−0.5	−0.5		−0.5
Other independent agencies	0.4	0.4	0.5	0.5		0.5	0.6	0.7		0.8
Export-Import Bank	−0.4	−0.5	−0.1	—		0.2	—	0.3		0.5
Tennessee Valley Authority	0.1	0.1	0.1	0.1		0.1	0.1	0.1		0.1
District of Columbia	0.1	0.1	0.1	0.1		0.2	0.1	0.1		0.2
Contingencies		0.4								
Total[d]	93.1	100.3	100.9	113.8	110.9	119.6	124.9	135.5	126.1	146.8
Interfund transactions	−0.5	−0.6	−0.8	−0.9	−0.9	−0.7	−0.9	−1.0	−1.0	−0.8
Total expenditures, administrative budget	92.6	99.7	109.0	113.0	110.0	119.0	124.0	134.5	125.0	146.0
Total expenditures as a percentage of GNP	16.3	14.8	14.9	14.7	14.3	15.4	13.5	13.3	12.4	14.5

a Includes military assistance.
b Includes international police force.
c Includes new research programs not otherwise allocated.
d Details may not add to totals due to rounding.

TABLE A-19. Models I and II: Expenditures from Federal Trust Funds, Selected Years, 1963–73

(In billions of current dollars for fiscal years)

Trust funds	Actual 1963	Proposed 1966	Projected 1968 Model I	Model II-A1	Model II-A2	Model II-B	Projected 1973 Model I	Model II-A1	Model II-A2	Model II-B
Department of Commerce	3.0	3.9	4.4	4.4	4.4	4.4	5.5	5.5		6.5
Department of Health, Education, and Welfare	15.8	20.4	23.3	24.4		25.2	29.5	35.6		39.1
Department of Labor	3.8	3.3	3.6	3.5		4.0	6.2	4.7		5.8
Other[a]	4.4	5.9	6.6	6.7	6.2	6.2	7.5	7.7	7.2	7.2
Interfund transactions	−0.5	−0.6	−0.9	−1.0		−0.8	−1.2	−1.0		−1.1
Total[b]	26.5	32.9	37.0	38.0	37.5	39.0	47.5	52.5	52.0	57.5
Trust fund expenditures as a percentage of GNP	4.7	4.8	5.0	4.9	4.9	5.1	5.2	5.2	5.2	5.7

[a] Includes the Veterans Administration, Defense Department (military), Civil Service Commission, Railroad Retirement Board, and other agencies.
[b] Details may not add to totals due to rounding.

TABLE A-20. Models I and II: Federal Government Expenditures, National Income Accounts, Selected Fiscal Years, 1963–73

(In billions of constant fiscal 1963 dollars)[a]

Item	Actual 1963	Proposed 1966	1968				1973			
			Model I	Model II-A1	Model II-A2	Model II-B	Model I	Model II-A1	Model II-A2	Model II-B
Purchases of goods and services	63.6	63.8	65.6	67.3	64.5	67.9	67.7	68.0	60.7	65.5
Transfer payments	29.2	33.7	38.6	39.9	39.9	41.9	45.9	53.4	53.4	63.6
Grants-in-aid to state and local governments	8.3	12.4	16.3	17.2	17.2	19.0	20.5	22.4	22.4	28.9
Net interest paid	7.4	8.2	8.8	8.8	8.8	8.9	8.7	9.0	9.0	9.2
Subsidies less current surplus of government enterprises	3.8	3.3	3.3	3.2	3.2	3.2	3.1	3.0	3.0	2.6
Total[b]	112.3	121.4	132.7	136.4	133.6	141.0	145.9	155.9	148.6	169.7
Expenditures as a percentage of GNP	19.8	18.6	19.3	19.1	18.7	19.7	18.1	18.0	17.1	19.5

Header spanning note: 1968 and 1973 columns fall under "Projected".

[a] For current dollar table, see Chap. VI, p. 80.
[b] Details may not add to totals due to rounding.

179

INDEX

Index

Accelerated public works program, 107, 112

Administrative budget: projections based on, 8, 39, 70, 72; data for 1900-64, 25-26, 28; limitations of, 40-42; Export-Import Bank operations, 99; Post Office Department, 111; labor and manpower, 125-27; transfers from general revenues to trust funds, 136-37; interest payments on government securities, 155

Adult education, 117

Africa, American aid in, 98

Agencies, federal: role of in budget-making, 37; role of in making budget projections, 15, 58-59

Agency for International Development, 86, 96-97

Agricultural programs, 76, 121, 141-43; reduction in, 11, 84

Agricultural Stabilization and Conservation Service, 141, 141n

Agriculture, Department of, 77, 96, 118, 132, 141-43; Forest Service, 103-04, 107, 141

Aid, foreign. *See* Agency for International Development; Alliance for Progress; Food-for-Peace program; Peace Corps

Air forces: conventional, 87, 91; continental defense, 90-91; troop carrier, 112

Air and missile defense forces, 90-91

Air pollution programs, 54

Alliance for Progress, 97-98

American Legion pension proposal, 140n

Anti-missile defense, 91

Antitrust Division. *See under* Justice, Department of

Apollo project, 101

Appalachia program, 109

Appropriation accounts, 40, 93

Appropriations legislation, 60

Area Redevelopment Administration, 108-09

Arms Control and Disarmament Agency, 86, 99

Arms reduction (*see also* Defense expenditures, reduction in; Model II-A2; Model II-B), 11, 67, 90, 92, 97

Army, U.S.: combat and support forces, 87, 91; airlift and tactical fighter programs, 91

Assumptions underlying projections (*see also under* various Models and individual programs): overall, 5, 25, 27, 67, 70, 73, 75, 157; Model I, 5-6, 8, 45, 58, 70, 73; Model II, 6-7, 16, 22, 45, 57-58; Model II-A, 7, 9, 11, 70-74; Model II-B, 7, 9, 11, 67, 70; nature of (*see also* Budget projections, nature of), 3-4, 43

Astronautics, 119

Astronomy, 54

Atmospheric sciences, 118

Atomic energy: peacetime uses of, 53, 94, 95, 157; defense-related activities, 94

Atomic Energy Commission, 86, 94-95, 118, civilian reactor program, 94

Balance-of-payments problem, 8

Berlin, 87

Bombers, long-range, 89

Bonneville Power Administration, 105

Break, George F., 40n

183

Impacted areas program, 114-15
Improvement factor, in social security benefits, 135, 136, 137n, 138
Income maintenance payments, 134
Income tax, individual. *See under* Taxes, federal
Incomes, taxable, ratio of debt to, 57
India, aid to, 97-98
Indian education services, 104n, 113
Industrialization and government responsibilities, 56
Inflation (*see also* Prices): effect on federal revenues and expenditures, 43; and the national debt, 56-57
Information Agency, U.S. *See* U.S. Information Agency
Intercontinental ballistic missiles, 89
Interest on national debt. *See under* Debt, national
Interior, Department of, 103-06, 113, 118, 153
Internal Revenue Service, 152
International affairs and finance, 51, 51n, 76, 86, 95-99, 141; as a percentage of gross national product, 98
International Development Association, 98
International Monetary Fund, 98
International organizations, memberships in and contributions to, 97-98
International police force, 97
International situation: assumptions concerning, 15, 21, 27, 87; effect of on federal budget, 21, 24, 27, 86-87; effect of on budget of National Aeronautics and Space Administration, 100
International transactions, effect of on federal budget, 36
Interstate Commerce Commission, 107n
Interstate highway program. *See under* Transportation.
Isotopes: uses of, 53; production and marketing of, 95

Job Corps (*see also* Economic Opportunity program; Poverty), 130
Johnson, President Lyndon B., 7, 58, 77, 135, 157

Joint Budget Committee, Congress, 60-61
Joint Economic Committee, Congress, 2, 2n
Judiciary, 150-51
Justice, Department of, 150, 152; Antitrust Division, 107n
Juvenile delinquency, 133

Korean War: effect of on federal expenditures and revenues, 24, 25, 31; government-business cooperation during, 53; payments to veterans of, 139-40
Krause, Lawrence B., 72n

Labor, Department of, 133, 150n, 154
Labor force: Model I, 6; Models II-A and II-B, 73-74
Labor-management relations, 126
Labor programs (*see also* Social insurance; Social security; Unemployment insurance), 57, 121, 125-28, 135n; Model I, 8, 74
Landsberg, Hans H., 107n
Lecht, Leonard A., 36n
Legislative Branch, 150-51
Leverage effect of government expenditures, 157
Library of Congress, 113, 117, 150n
Loan guarantees and insurance, 13, 22, 39-41, 53, 54, 109, 116, 141, 146, 147
Loans, repayment of, as offset to expenditures, 40-41
Lunar landing, manned, 100

Manned space flight program, 101
Manpower Administration, 126-27
Manpower development and training (*see also* Education and training programs; Work and training programs), 125-27
Marine Corps, 91
Mariner program, 101
Maritime Administration, 110
Maternal and child health care, 122n, 125
McNamara, Robert S., 87